Soft Fruit Growing

BY

H. G. Witham Fogg

JUPITER: LONDON

First published in 1979 by
JUPITER BOOKS (LONDON) LIMITED
167 Hermitage Road London N4 1LZ.

Copyright © H. G. Witham Fogg 1979.

ISBN 0 906379 01 6

Composed on the Linotype-Paul VIP in 11-point Garamond and printed and bound
in Great Britain by Tonbridge Printers Limited at their Peach Hall Works,
Tonbridge, Kent.

Soft Fruit Growing

Contents

Chapter One : Growing Your Own Fruit

WHILE ALL FORMS OF GARDENING CAN BE SATISFY-ing there is a real sense of achievement when one is able to go into the garden to pick fruit of one's own growing. Even allowing for a little permissable imagination there is no doubt that home-grown fruit does taste better than that bought in shops and which may have been gathered quite a long time previously.

Anyone who has never had the pleasure of sampling freshly gathered strawberries or raspberries will hardly be able to realize how superior such fruit is to that which has had to travel and which.has not been allowed to remain on the bushes to obtain the full size and flavour. In addition the gardener has the joy each year of being able to see the leafless branches of winter gradually unfold their leaves and then make posies of flowers in which bees become busy.

While all aspects of gardening can become a relaxing occupation, easing workaday tensions, fruit growing brings its own rich reward in making it possible to produce tasty and health-promoting crops without any difficult-to-master techniques being involved.

There is no real problem in growing good crops of soft fruit in ordinary small gardens where a large orchard cannot be established. Selection of varieties is important for it is easy to chose particular sorts because we happen to like their flavour or appearance, whereas they may be quite unsuitable for the conditions we have available.

We know now a lot about rootstocks and the effect they have on subsequent growth. Specific information can always be obtained on contacting the Research Stations concerning any particular problem. It pays to buy from one of the many reputable nursery firms, preferably one which specializes in fruit culture. Fortunately the large majority of soft fruit bushes are grown on their own stock so that the question of grafting does not arise.

It is possible to plant fruit hedges, and gooseberries and currants can be used for this purpose. These subjects can also be trained as espaliers or single cordons and used for growing beside paths or in order to divide one part of the garden from another. It is also possible to grow currants, gooseberries, figs and grape-vines in large pots or tubs, while cultivated blackberries and loganberries are very suitable for growing against a wall or fence where they become both ornamental and productive.

To grow good fruit it is essential to prepare the ground well for the bushes will remain in the same position for some years. It is, therefore, worth spending time and effort in soil preparation, incorporating rotted manure, compost and other humus-forming matter. Make the holes large enough for the root to be spread out fully and do not plant too deeply. Use the soil mark on the stems as a guide to depth of planting with an extra few centimetres to allow for soil sinkage. Plant firmly and retread the soil around the bushes from time to time until a new root system has formed.

Fruiting plants grow best in full sunshine, even in partial shade growth will not be so vigorous and the crop smaller. All excepting blueberries grow best in a soil just slightly acid — pH 5.5 — 6.5. Blueberries thrive in soil which is more acid, say pH 4.8 — 5.0.

Planting time for fruit bushes and canes is from late October until early April according to soil and weather conditions. Never plant when the soil is frostbound, wet or sticky. If items ordered from a nurseryman arrive when they cannot be put into their growing positions, they can be kept for some days with roots protected in a shed or greenhouse or be heeled into a temporary position until the soil is workable.

Chapter Two : Consider The Soil

SOIL IS THE GARDENER'S STOCK-IN-HAND. IT IS NOT dead, inert material but contains myriads of living organisms which help crops to grow. All soils have reserves of the plant foods required by fruit trees and bushes but the addition of essential elements will improve the resulting crop tremendously. There are of course, many types of soil including, loamy, sandy, chalky or limey, clay and peaty, but undoubtedly the best soil for producing fruit is one containing plenty of humus, that blackish, crumbly material.

Where the soil is naturally chalky, plants may suffer from chlorosis or the yellowing of the leaves resulting in poor growth. Sandy soil dries out quickly, while clay soil often settles down like cement. The working in of humus-forming material or ripe compost will improve all these soils and make it easier for the necessary fibrous roots to develop. For too long, instead of feeding the soil we have been content to feed the plants and in doing so have often relied on powder or artificial fertilizers. These may stimulate growth for a time but their continued use leads to thin, lifeless, impoverished soil.

Failing animal manure, ripe compost, spent hops, peat, leaf mould, seaweed, fish manure, meat and bone meal, poultry manure and hoof and horn meal are all good. They encourage even, non-forcing growth. Water is also vital and is lost from the soil in a variety of ways. Transpiration probably accounts for the greatest loss. Water is not held indefinitely in the plants, but moved through the tissues carrying food and is liberated through green tissues, especially the leaves. There are many thousands of them scattered over the average fruit plant.

In addition to water, other materials are liberated through these outlets, but water is the most important and in the greatest bulk. A large amount of water is needed in the soil to sustain even a small plant such as a strawberry. Much greater is the amount needed by trees such as cherries.

It is also true that the healthier the plants and the better-fed they are the more moisture will be required. Direct evaporation from the soil is also an important source of loss and is greatest when sun and wind interact to dry the surface, especially over a period of days and weeks. Soil constantly cultivated will lose more moisture by evaporation than one which is cultivated less frequently, except where cracking results.

The aim should be to carry out any major cultivations during the winter rather than leave this until the spring when the opportunities for doing the job are fewest and the moisture-loss by evaporation very often the greatest. Generalization is often dangerous, but in the main it would seem that, if winter cultivations can be properly carried out, those done in spring need only be of a surface nature so that as soon as possible a fine surface tilth is created.

Mulching is the natural way of conserving soil moisture. Good weed control before applying the mulch is important since the idea of complete cover to a reasonable depth will cut down the need for weeding. Even so, some weeds will grow through the mulch and these can either be pulled out or killed by spraying. Straw mulches can be maintained as a permanent feature in a plantation, particularly on light or gravelly soil, but fire risk with complete straw coverage must be considered.

Other forms of mulches already mentioned do supply plant foods and have much to commend them but unfortunately they do not let through into the subsoil anything like the amount of moisture that straw does. They often cake hard in summer, shedding moisture or even evaporating much of what rain has fallen. They do however, rot down fairly quickly and may have to be replaced once during the summer.

Non-feeding types of mulches include peat, sawdust, bark fibre, wood shavings and similar waste products. In none of these is moisture allowed to go through to the subsoil and they contain little or no available plant foods. In addition sawdust and wood shavings can leach out nitrogen rather quickly.

[10]

Against that, many give excellent weed cover provided they are put on to an adequate depth, say 5 cm (2 in). Sawdust has been used with success by a number of growers who find it easy to come by, but it is a mistake to use it repeatedly, especially in view of the danger of the loss of good soil structure near the surface.

Various forms of bark fibre have also been used as mulches and here again, instances have occurred where soil structure has been damaged as a result of generous and repeated treatment. Bark fibre is now available in large quantities and there is a need for observation to discover what this material can do and how it can be used to the best advantage.

Mulches are definitely valuable to the fruit grower but must be used carefully. Some possible disadvantages attendant on their use should be borne in mind. Straw for example may encourage vermin and the grower could find that the bark of his trees has been girdled by vermin feeding and the first thing he notices is that the tree looks unhealthy and is producing few new shoots. Another point is that mulches, particularly those of an organic nature, should not be heaped round the tree. Whatever is used should be spread at least to the extent of the branches and probably a bit more. The area immediately round the main stem should be cleared for about 15 cm (6 in.) so that damage is avoided.

Iron deficiency either alone or combined with manganese shortage is not uncommon in some fruit trees and bushes. This is more likely to show when the bushes are growing in limey soil. The most obvious sign of iron shortage is the yellowing of the foliage especially the younger leaves during late summer and autumn.

A good way of maintaining healthy young fruit bushes is to lightly prick into the surface soil around each specimen a dressing of fish manure. This contains a high percentage of potash, phosphates and nitrogen. Do this in December and as an alternative, apply farmyard manure as a summer mulch.

Chapter Three : Propagation

THE GARDENER WHO WANTS TO PLANT JUST A FEW
fruit trees and bushes will not perhaps be much concerned with
propagation. There are a good many suppliers of first class trees and
bushes in this country and generally speaking one may very safely leave
the question of raising stocks to them.

There is no doubt however, that one of the most fascinating sides of
fruit growing is the propagation of your own planting stock. Very often
this enables one to grow varieties which are scarce or difficult to obtain
through the normal channels.

There is in operation, a registration scheme sponsored by the Ministry
of Agriculture, Fisheries and Food. Certificates are issued to those
growers whose stocks have been inspected by the Ministry's officials and
were found to be healthy and true at the time of inspection. This applies
especially to black currants, raspberries, and strawberries. Such precau-
tions reduce the possibility of the spread of virus and other diseases
particularly in raspberries and strawberries.

However healthy may be the stock one obtains, if there are growing in
nearby gardens trees or plants affected by disease it can and usually does
soon spread to healthy specimens. Aphides and similar sucking insects
are largely the cause of the increase of virus and other diseases. Growing
plants under healthy conditions will usually lessen the incidence of
disease. It is very noticeable that where animal manure and compost are
used in preference to purely chemical fertilizers there is more resistance
to breakdown. In addition, weak sappy plants seem the most likely target
for pest attacks.

However good the subsequent cultivation and pruning of fruit bushes may be, if they have been propagated from inferior stock crops are bound to be poor in quantity and quality. It is possible to propagate from virus infected strawberries and raspberries and from black currants suffering from reversion. However, apart from the indifferent appearance of the young stock produced, there will be little or no fruit.

Soft fruits such as currants and gooseberries, raspberries and blackberries are nearly always propagated from cuttings so that grafting or incompatibility troubles do not arise. Even so, the biggest single contribution to the successful growing of soft fruit is the health of the planting stock. Since the average life of a plantation of currants and gooseberries could be anything from ten to twenty years, the importance of starting with a good stock will be realized.

Cultivated blackberries and loganberries are easy to propagate in the autumn by pulling down healthy stems and rooting the tips by weighing them down so that they are in close contact with the soil. Once rooted, the tips are severed and then grown on as separate plants.

The raising of melons, strawberries and tomatoes will be found detailed under their respective headings.

Chapter Four: Pruning Trees and Bushes

It is one thing to build up shapely trees or to buy them from a nurseryman but quite another to keep them not only of good shape but with branches that regularly bear fruit. Pruning not only regulates the quantity, but very often the quality, of the fruit. Unpruned fruit trees are very liable to become a mass of tangled branches with a crowded centre and with fruit produced irregularly, and very often with large trees, at the top of the branches.

Cutting should be done so that the balance of the tree or bush is preserved and this will allow air and sun to reach all parts of the tree, which is so essential if a continuous supply of fruit buds is to develop. Then, of course, with good-shaped trees, spraying and fruit gathering are made much easier.

Before making a cut the pruner should not only think of the wood he is removing but of the new shoot that is going to become the leader or fruit spur. This means cutting immediately above a well-placed bud and one which is not going to grow straight into another branch. Good tools are essential for any and every gardening operation if it is to be done properly. It is certainly so in the case of pruning. Whether a knife, or secateurs are used, clean cuts must always be made. This will mean quicker healing of the wound and less likelihood of disease spores entering and gaining a hold.

It is not possible to give cut and dried directions either by word or diagram to show how every tree should be pruned. Each tree is an individual and one method is not suitable for all fruits or for that matter for all trees of the same family.

We can assume that even with a three or four-year-old bush or tree,

[14]

there has been some shaping. This simply means making sure that the branches are in the right positions for if they are wrong when the trees are young, they will if not dealt with, still be wrong when the tree is old.

By comparing a well-trained orchard tree with one allowed to grow anyhow, it will be obvious that training by pruning is necessary. Bushes and standards should have an open centre so that sun and light act on the inside growths just the same as they do on the outside.

It is possible to over-prune and many amateur gardeners do so, for it is not always necessary to cut back to the old wood. There should be an object in making a cut. Before attempting to prune at all, one should consider the subject being dealt with. A point worth remembering is that usually the pruning of really strong growing trees will encourage more vigour. Conversely, it is the slow, thin growing varieties that usually benefit from hard pruning.

However efficiently pruning is carried out, it will not in itself ensure a good crop of fruit. The stock on which the trees are grafted or budded has a tremendous effect on the fruiting ability, while general cultivation including feeding will also influence the crop.

Chapter Five: Alphabetical List of Fruit: Including Full Cultural Information

BLACKBERRY

Among the most accommodating fruits for the small, as well as the larger garden, is the blackberry and its allied hybrids. Apart from their heavy cropping, these most useful plants can be utilized for covering unsightly fences or for screening an untidy corner of the garden, or for dividing one part of the plot from another.

They certainly need some kind of support over which the long growths can be trained. While they can be planted in shady positions, for heavy crops of well-ripened fruit, they need an open but not exposed, sunny position so that the fruit ripens properly.

Although not really particular as to soil, drainage should be good and in preparing the site, it is advisable to move the ground deeply and if humus is lacking, work in a good application of decayed manure. Failing this, any other bulky matter such as peat, leaf mould, and spent hops can be used. To these add seaweed fertilizer, fish meal or bone meal which will provide feeding over a long period. Unless the ground is naturally limey finish off by dressing the surface soil with hydrated lime, at the rate of 113 g (4 oz.) to the square metre.

Where more than one blackberry bush is being grown, it is advisable to space them at least 3 m (9 ft.) apart For supports where a screen is being formed, posts standing up to 2 m (6 ft.) above ground level, are very suitable. Three strands of taut wire should be run between the posts at 60 cm (2 ft.) intervals. Such supports will be suitable for the most strong growing varieties as well as for those that are less rampant.

Nurserymen usually supply blackberries as strong one-year-old specimens and send them out from November to early April. They

[16]

should be planted immediately on arrival although in the event of the soil being sticky or frost-bound, they can be 'heeled in' until conditions improve. Make sure to spread the roots out and plant firmly, retreading the soil around the stems from time to time, since frosts often loosen the ground.

Once they are planted, the canes should be shortened to about 1 m (3 ft.) and tied loosely to the supports. When it is obvious the plants are beginning to grow in the spring, it is best to shorten the canes to about 23–25 cm (9–10 in.) from ground level, cutting immediately above a stout bud.

Such action will lead to the production of strong young fruiting canes for the following season. If, however, fruit is required the first year the second shortening of the growths should not be carried out and initially, the canes need not be cut back so severely. This will mean less shapely plants and the probability that the following season's growth (or some of it) will develop from the older canes instead of coming from the base. It is when stems come from ground level that they are easier to train and the fruit is better, while the annual pruning can be done more easily with less tangling of the stems.

Pruning of established blackberries consists of cutting out the old canes and tying in the new ones, which will bear fruit the following season. Any superfluous canes, that is those that cannot be conveniently tied in or would lead to overcrowding should be cut right out.

Varieties

Ashton Cross as the name suggests, was selected at the Research Station. Of real blackberry flavour the freely bearing berries are large, and of good appearance. Although of vigorous growth, it is not as thick or prickly as most others.

Bedford Giant raised by Laxtons has very early, sweet and juicy berries which are attractive-looking with fewer seeds than most.

Black Diamond is strong growing and of similar habit to the Himalayan variety and has been found first class for preserving.

Blowers has particularly large jet-black berries produced over many weeks. It makes upright growth and is particularly useful for growing where space is limited.

[17]

B

Edward Langley is not so well known as it ought to be, for its vigorous growth carries large crops of extra good flavoured berries early in the season.

Himalayan Giant is one of the best known blackberries. Said to have come from the mountains of the same name, it is probably the strongest growing of all and since it bears on both old and new wood, it is an enormous cropper of very large fruit. Excellent for cooking and preserving it is inclined to be 'seedy'. To keep the plants within bounds, they should be pruned annually.

John Innes Hybrid is a most valuable late variety and a heavy bearer, the fruit being of good appearance and particularly sweet and juicy and containing few seeds. Of rather a bushy habit of growth, it is well worth growing.

Merton Thornless is another worth while sort ripening in mid-August, and continuing to bear over a long period, the large sweet fruit being most freely produced. The compact growth is entirely thornless which therefore gives this variety an appeal which some others do not possess.

The *Parsley-leaved* variety is a form of the common English blackberry. It is widely grown on account of its fine fruit and good appearance. The foliage is quite ornamental being deeply cut and since it is of moderate growth, this variety is often used for growing on trellis-work etc.

Dewberries are of American origin. The canes die back after fruiting, and it is therefore best to remove the old stems once the berries are gathered, to encourage the new basal growths to develop. The very large berries are glossy black with little core.

Smoothstem is a variety raised in Maryland, U.S.A. and the breeding programme involved the use of Merton Thornless and an American variety named Eldorado. The plant is vigorous-growing, entirely thornless with no tendency at all to revert to prickles. It is late-maturing, ripening from very late August until October. The freely produced fruits are of good size.

Wilson Junior, of American origin, is another sort with an upright habit of growth, the good sized fruit being of attractive appearance and flavour.

BLUEBERRY *(Vaccinium corymbosum)*

The name 'blueberry' covers several species of *vaccinium* but does not include *Vaccinium myrtillus*, which is the correct name of the whortleberry.

The real blueberries are the finest varieties of the Highbush type such as are grown on a very large scale in North America. They thrive in moist, acid soil where often little else will flourish but they will not stand drought conditions. For complete success, the soil should contain an abundance of humus with moisture always available, although a waterlogged top soil will not be tolerated.

Treated well and pruned regularly, the bushes can be kept to a height of about 2 m (6 ft.). Under good conditions they can be retained in fruiting condition for fifteen years or more. Apart from their fruiting value, blueberries are ornamental in the autumn when the leaves assume most lovely colourings.

An open, sunny situation should be chosen. It is well worth preparing the soil for such long-lived plants. Do this well in advance of planting time. Small plants move best and specimens supplied by the growers are usually no more than 15–30 cm (6–12 in.) high.

To allow for future development, they should be spaced up to 2 m apart each way. Newly planted bushes should be mulched with good compost or decayed manure and peat. In subsequent years, a good, early, spring top-dressing will prove beneficial but lime in any form must be avoided.

Little pruning is necessary for the first couple of years after planting. Subsequently, the older, thicker stems are cut out to encourage basal growths. The white bell-shaped flowers are borne on the previous season's growth. They appear from March onwards and are resistant to frost damage. The fruit ripens from July to September and established bushes will bear up to 2 kilos (4–5 lb) each year. It is important to let the fruit mature on the bushes where it will remain in good condition for some days. Ripe berries are a dark bluish colour at the stem end. A reddish tinge indicates immaturity.

General cultivation is simple and apart from keeping the ground clean there is nothing to do although birds should be kept off when the fruit is ripening. Netting is useful for this purpose.

[19]

Apart from wild plants, from which heavy crops can often be gathered, there are a number of good named hybrids now being grown in Britain. These give a prolonged ripening period. Some are of American origin although many have been well tested at Long Ashton Research Station. Among the best are the following:

Berkeley, of spreading habit with large pale-blue berries in branched clusters.

Blueray, of strong upright growth with tight clusters of large berries.

Earliblue, with strong upright growth and large berries ripening from mid-July.

Jersey, although an older variety, is good, producing long open sprays of large fruit.

In Holland and Germany research workers have long been busily engaged in breeding improved varieties and many experts believe that blueberries can be developed into a really worthwhile crop.

BOYSENBERRY

The exact parentage of this hybrid is unknown but it seems quite probable that its ancestors include the blackberry, loganberry and raspberry. The fruit is like a fatter loganberry but a dark wine colour, not too seedy with a sharper flavour and a softer core. It is a vigorous grower producing its fruit on twigs well set out from the main stems making it easier and more comfortable to pick. It is a splendid fruit for jam. Quite hardy, the boysenberry grows well against a wall or fence.

CAPE GOOSEBERRY *(Physalis peruviana)*

Often referred to as 'golden berries' these plants are able to produce at least two or three pounds of excellent fruit in late summer. While they have been known and grown for many years it is the plants raised from a clone selected by the Long Ashton Research Station that has made this subject reliable and worth cultivating. *Physalis peruviana* will grow in most soils, but are best not planted in rich ground since this encourages excessive leafy growth and hinders fruiting.

In February or March, in a temperature of 18°–20°C. (65°–70°F.), plants can be raised by sowing seeds shallowly in pans of light compost. When danger of cold weather is past, the plants can be moved to the cold frame before moving them to their outdoor positions which for preference, should be sheltered and free from cold winds.

[20]

If desired, the plants can be given larger pots, say the 20–23 cm (8–9 in.) size, and be allowed to fruit in these in the greenhouse or outdoors. The advantage of growing them in pots is that they can be given protection from bad weather as necessary, and those outside can be taken into the greenhouse in the autumn to continue the fruit-ripening process. Water the plants frequently during dry weather, and if side-shoots have not developed by the time the plants are 30 cm (1 ft.) high, take out the growing points to encourage laterals to form. This will encourage bushy habit otherwise the plants might grow tall and a little cumbersome. Fruiting specimens of up to 90 cm (3 ft.) high are an impressive sight. Particularly in dry weather and in the case of greenhouse plants, the stems should be lightly tapped when the flowers are opening. This distributes the pollen and aids fertilization and fruit setting. The careful removal of badly placed shoots will keep the plants shapely.

There are unlikely to be any cultural problems and the only pests liable to appear are greenfly which can be controlled by spraying with derris or pyrethrum. Special attention should be given to the growing points and to the calyx ridges where the pests sometimes settle. An occasional spraying of a good fungicide will normally keep the plants in a healthy condition.

The fruit develops inside parchment-like husks which break easily to expose the golden berries. If left inside the dry husks, the fruit remains in good condition for several months.

Once all the fruit has been harvested the stems can be cut down to ground level. If you decide to leave the plants in the open ground for the winter they should be covered with a layer of straw or similar material removing this in April according to weather conditions.

CHINESE GOOSEBERRY (*Actinidia chinensis*)

This has been grown in Britain for many years but it is still quite a novelty as a fruit producing plant. Years ago a quantity of the fruit was imported from New Zealand and at various times it has been offered in the London markets.

A climbing plant, in appearance this subject can be compared with a large-sized vigorous grape-vine growing up to 8 m (24 ft.) annually, although if the height is restricted, the crop will be larger. The chinese gooseberry is a dioecious plant, which means that only the female plants produce fruit. The presence of male flowers is essential for fertilization, one male plant being sufficient to pollinate eight females. The flowers will have to be hand-pollinated and the plants liquid-fed at regular intervals during the summer.

The large ornamental heart-shaped leaves will be a credit to any pergola, arch, trellis or wall, and the attractive flowers appear in May and June. Once the flowers have set, the fruits develop rapidly from July onwards. They should be gathered in November, when the leaves begin to fall and if kept in store, they will progressively ripen throughout the winter. Ripe fruit will remain in good condition in a refrigerator for up to six weeks.

The 'gooseberries' are reddish-brown in colour and about the size of a small pullet's egg, the flesh being soft, white and juicy. They should be peeled and eaten fresh for dessert with cream, or stewed or used for decoration. The fruit has a slightly acid flavour and is considered to have great nutritional value. By comparison with a lemon, it is three or four times richer in vitamin C. This is why in China it is known as the 'Tree of Health' and the consumption of the fruit there is valued by and for elderly and sick people.

The chinese gooseberry will thrive best in any well-drained soil and as for most plants, a generous application of bulky organic manure, garden compost or peat, will prove beneficial when forked into the surface of the soil prior to planting. Since it is a true climbing plant it should be planted against a fence or wall having supports on which the vines can climb. A south-facing situation is ideal. Exposed sites should be avoided. Plant at least 6 m (15 ft.) apart.

Chinese gooseberries will do exceptionally well grown in large containers, 30 cm (12 in.) pots, under glass. A heated glasshouse is not necessary.

Pruning is necessary when the plants are sufficiently developed and should be carried out in December or January. Prune above the last bud which bore fruit during the preceding year. In the spring, this bud will develop into a branch which will in turn bear fruit and the following winter will be pruned in the same way again.

Seed is sometimes available and can be sown under heated glass early in the year, the seedlings being pricked-off and potted-up in the usual way. Subsequently, they can be planted outdoors in sheltered positions.

CURRANTS

1. *Black Currant (Ribes nigrum)*

It is believed that the name 'currant' is derived from Corinth, a famous city of ancient Greece. Currants and raisins are still imported from that country but they belong to the genus *vitis* while the currant of our gardens belongs to the genus *ribes*.

The black currant is among the most important of the soft fruits, it is rich in vitamin C, even more so than oranges. This is why black currant juice is so widely used as a drink today. Several firms now require this fruit on a large scale and provide market growers with long-term contracts for the production of the berries. Many tons of black currants are used to make 'Ribena' the health drink which helps to strengthen resistance against colds, influenza and other infections. Some experts reckon that the variety Baldwin has the highest vitamin C content. Black currant tea is effective for curing colds. The fruit can be used in many other ways and is appreciated by most people in the form of jam, jelly and syrup, while it is tempting in pies and puddings.

Heavy yields can be expected from healthy established bushes which will normally bear well for at least twelve or fifteen years. This crop succeeds in almost all types of soil, excepting in thin chalky land. Ideally, a deep loamy soil having a high organic content should be provided. This will ensure moisture is retained even during long spells of dry weather. Black currants certainly like moisture during the growing and fruiting season but stodgy cold, clay soil will not produce the heaviest crops. Such ground can be made more suitable by working in compost and well-rotted manure.

The situation is also of some importance. If the bushes are exposed to cold north and east winds, insect activity will be discouraged and this is needed to distribute the pollen and thus ensure a good set of fruit. In this connection the bushes should be planted where they are not in a frost pocket or otherwise exposed to frosts when the flowers are opening.

The selection of the site and the preparation of the soil should be done

[23]

well before planting time. Then comes the choosing of varieties. While these are described a little later it cannot be over-emphasized that only the best quality, named varieties should be grown. Never buy from doubtful sources, for there are many first class fruit specialists who have their reputation to consider and whose stock is wholly dependable.

At one time black currants were a bit 'chancy' with Big Bud and reversion being rife. Now, because of the scheme worked out by the Ministry of Agriculture, leading fruit specialists supply certified bushes. No such scheme can completely ensure that the planting material is one hundred per cent free from possible troubles but it does give the buyer confidence that he is starting with really good stock.

It is most satisfactory to buy two year-old bushes. These will normally have three or four shoots and will become established more quickly than older specimens. One year-old specimens are sometimes offered. They will be longer in coming into bearing and it is not so easy to see any 'rogues' at that age. Against this of course, if the cuttings were taken from certified stock there should be little fear of Big Bud Mite. By the time a bush is two years old the presence of any reversion will have shown.

Although black currants can be planted from late October until the end of March, early planting is best and for preference it should be done in November. It is advisable to cut down newly planted bushes to within 5 cm (2 in.) of their base in the February after planting. A distance of 1.5 m (5 ft.) should be allowed between bushes and rows. On fairly large scale planting, what is known as the hedge system of planting is carried out. In this, the bushes are spaced 90 cm (3 ft.) apart with 2.40 m (8 ft.) or more between the rows. This allows for the mechanical cleaning of the land. Even then, it is none too wide when spreading varieties such as *Wellington XXX,* are being grown.

One way of keeping down weeds which is largely practised in parts of East Anglia and possibly elsewhere too, is to cover the whole of the ground around and between the bushes with straw or rushes. This decaying litter acts as a weed smother and helps to retain moisture in the soil.

To replace the nitrogen taken from the ground by the rotting straw, a good dressing of a nitrogenous fertilizer should be applied very early each spring. This fertilizer will be washed in by the rains. It is usual to top up the decaying straw each year to maintain a good blanket effect. The only weeds likely to appear are those strong perennials which are powerful enough to push up through the straw. Shortage of potash in the soil shows by the edges of the leaves becoming scorched. An annual mulch of manure, compost or straw helps in preventing mineral deficiencies.

It is of course, possible to partially straw-mulch the beds or bushes. This simply implies placing the straw around the bushes, leaving the space between the rows uncovered. This means that there will be little or no hand-weeding required near the bushes while mechanical cleaning can be carried out between the rows.

It is not satisfactory to grow other crops between the rows of black currants, for apart from all other considerations, the bushes make a fairly widespread, near the surface, root system. The necessary cultivation needed for inter-cropping, would mean a risk of damage to the roots of the bushes with a marked loss of crop. Some growers have tried grassing down the spaces between the rows, but so far no advantages have been noted from this method. Since the grass needs cutting at intervals from June to October more work is involved. Many growers find that an annual thick mulch of farmyard manure placed round the bushes leads to the heaviest crops.

Black currants must be pruned annually. The object being to encourage the production of new wood, preferably from the base. There should be no forming a 'leg' or central stem, all shoots should arise from the soil. The first year after planting, bushes are cut down to ground level. This will result in a good supply of new shoots during the summer and autumn.

Black currants bear fruit on their new, light coloured wood. Unpruned bushes produce only a small amount of new wood, usually at the ends of the branches. This leads to unproductive bushes with much unwanted old, basal wood. Older branches should be cut back to young strong shoots. The dark colour of the old wood makes it easy to determine which is the new growth.

Proper soil conditions and a sufficiency of feeding matter in the ground is the right way to build up plenty of fruit-producing branches, but regular systematic pruning is required if a good crop in weight and quality is to be produced annually. A few varieties which are of a spreading habit, produce their branches very near the ground. These will have to be cut right out or where possible, pruned back to an upright growing shoot.

Some gardeners prune their black currants in winter, when of course one can see all the growths clearly, but the best time for the job is in September, when fruit picking has been completed. This early pruning saves the bushes wasting their strength on shoots which will be cut out later and, more important, next season's fruiting wood is able to ripen much better.

By growing several varieties it is possible to lengthen the picking season and thus avoid a glut. This of course applies where a fair number of bushes are involved. Another important point is that some varieties hang longer in good condition on the bushes. They are the same ones which last better in wet weather. Among the best of these are *Seabrook's Black, Baldwin* and *Westwick Choice*.

The berries should be picked on the 'strig' and not separately. They can of course easily be 'strigged' indoors with a table fork. Time of picking is important for sometimes the berries look ripe before they are. Once the top berries on the strig have softened harvesting should begin. If gathered too early a lot of weight may be lost, for in the last few days of maturing the berries rapidly increase in size and moisture content.

It is not often that all the berries on individual bushes are ready at the same time and it is usually necessary to go over the bushes more than once. If fruit is being marketed it must be picked when quite dry or mildew and other troubles will develop. For small quantities, one- or two-pound punnets can be used, for larger amounts six-pound chip baskets are best.

Diseases

Reversion is a virus disease which causes changes in the growth of affected bushes. It can completely prevent cropping and is incurable. Once it affects a bush there is no point in waiting to see the result. The bush should be burned immediately. Clean stock can only be maintained by regular inspection of the bushes and by discarding any looking 'suspicious'. Propagate only from really healthy specimens.

Symptoms of reversion first become noticeable in June and it is wise to look over the bushes at the end of that month. The disease can be identified by the distinct appearance of the leaves. A healthy leaf has at least five veins and the edges are finely serrated. In an infected leaf, the number of veins will be less than five and in bad cases the leaf will resemble that of an oak. A reverted bush will often grow very strongly. This is partly due to the fact that no fruit is set. The strength of the bush therefore goes into extra wood production.

The dried up 'strig' without berries is easily seen and this condition is often known as 'running off'. Since the virus is in the cell sap, it will be obvious why there can be no cure and why too, it is necessary to deal with the Big Bud Mite which can so easily spread the disease.

Pests

In order to keep black currants healthy a certain amount of routine spraying is necessary. Winter spraying with tar oil or D.N.C. will control hibernating greenfly and other aphides. It will also do away with various fungi which sometimes attack the bushes. *Green Capsid Bug,* sometimes known as *Lygus Bug,* occasionally attacks the foliage and shoots, interfering with normal growth with the leaves becoming pale. A mixed tar oil and petroleum wash will clear this pest which attacks other fruit bushes as well.

The worst pest to affect black currants is the *Gall Mite,* usually referred to as the *Big Bud Mite.* It is very tiny and can only be seen under a microscope. It lives inside the buds which is why it is difficult to control. By its feeding methods it causes the buds to swell and produce the easily recognized condition known as Big Bud. Unfortunately however, mites may be in buds which are not swollen.

They are active from March onwards and although they have no wings they are carried from bush to bush by wind currents. They may also settle on red currants, the flowering currant and on gooseberries, which are often unsuspected hosts. In July, the mites enter the buds, begin to breed and then hibernate. It is usually in August that one can see the first swollen buds, although they are more readily noticed after the leaves have fallen. Control of the Gall Mite is essential not only because of the

[27]

direct harm it does, but because it is the vector of the incurable virus disease known as reversion.

The mite can fortunately be controlled by spraying with a two per cent lime-sulphur spray at the 'grape' stage of flowering, followed by two further applications at fortnightly intervals. A few varieties, notably Goliath, are sulphur-shy and are liable to leaf scorch. For these it is best to use the lime-sulphur at a strength of one per cent.

Caterpillar and *Leaf Curling Midge* can be checked by adding Draza when applying the lime-sulphur wash. *Weevils* can do minor damage to the foliage, while *Currant Eelworm* will spoil leaf buds. Sometimes the *Currant Shoot Borer* becomes active. This caterpillar bores into the stems in the spring, causing the leaves to wilt and the shoot to die back. It then pupates in the tunnel during the spring and the moth emerges some weeks afterwards. Eggs are laid on little cuts made in the fruit and later the caterpillar can be found inside the berries feeding on the seeds. It usually leaves the fruit in early July making little cocoons on the branches, remaining there during the winter. This is why it is so important not to neglect the tar oil washes, for these sprayings will destroy the Currant Borer and many other pests.

Propagation

The easiest way to propagate black currants is by taking cuttings in the autumn. It is also possible to increase stock by using soft wood cuttings in summer and by layering some of the lower branches.

Autumn hardwood cuttings should be made from sturdy one year-old shoots from the best healthy bushes, certified the previous summer. To propagate from any old bushes is asking for trouble. The cuttings should be 20–23 cm (8–9 in.) long and trimmed neatly to a bud top and bottom. Select a well-drained position if possible on the sandy side where the land is in good heart and which preferably was manured for a previous crop. Take out a trench and insert the cuttings well down 15–17 cm (6–7 in.) apart with only a couple of buds showing. That means the cuttings will be buried in the soil 15 cm (6 in.) or more. When returning the soil to the trench, make sure that the cuttings are really firm.

This deep planting encourages the growth of basal shoots and lessens the possibility of a 'leg' forming. If more than one trench is necessary they should be 60 cm (2 ft.) apart. Different varieties should be clearly marked. It has been found that freshly-taken cuttings root much better than those taken some time before being put in the ground.

Soft wood cuttings taken in July are more trouble. Terminal shoots about 8 cm (3 in.) long are selected and are prepared in the normal way. Insert them in a closed and shaded frame, giving overhead sprayings of water to prevent wilting. Rooting will take place within three or four weeks. Air can then be admitted and gradually the frame lights can be left off. The rooted cuttings can be planted out in the autumn and left in that position for a year, before being moved to their fruiting positions.

Varieties

Choice of varieties is wide but the actual number worth growing by the gardener is comparatively small. For the average grower the following can be depended upon.

Amos Black An erratic variety in regard to yields, its greatest value being that it is late, thus providing a longer season.

Baldwin One of the best maincrops, it forms a compact upright bush. It responds well to good feeding but does not like really heavy soils.

Boskoop Giant An established early variety which colours evenly and is not prone to splitting. Rather tall-growing, it becomes leggy if not pruned regularly. Mendip Cross is sometimes preferred to this variety.

Cotswold Cross Tall growing, its yield lessens after two or three years.

Daniel's September A good flavoured heavy cropper, but variable in growth the fruit often being at different stages of ripeness on the same bush.

Malvern Cross This fairly tall grower is sometimes very heavy cropping with much lighter yields the following season.

Mendip Cross An early variety of great vigour. The large fruit appears on long strigs making picking easy. Similar to Boskoop Giant, it is often grown instead of that variety.

Raven A vigorous grower usually cropping heavily, the good-sized berries being well-flavoured.

Seabrook's Black or *French Black* An old variety which crops well. It is sometimes shy in producing basal growths.

Silvergeiter An early variety with large fruit on long strigs. It is not always easy to obtain.

Tinker Not often listed by nurserymen, this is quite a good mid-season variety.

Wellington XXX A heavy cropping mid-season variety. Growth is vigorous but occasionally sprawling, although with careful pruning this habit can be adjusted.

Among other varieties which do not seem to be in general cultivation are *Blacksmith, Davisons Eight, Laxton's Giant, Laxton's Grape, Supreme, Victoria* and *Wallace Seedling*.

2. Red Currants

Red currants are not nearly so popular as black currants, although they are used for jam, jelly and pies, while there is some demand for them on the part of canners who sometimes mix them with raspberries.

The origin of the red currant as we know it, is somewhat confused but it is generally reckoned that three species have contributed to the constitution of present day varieties. These are *Ribes vulgare, Ribes rubrum* and *Ribes petraeum*.

The bushes grow well on ordinary good soils but they dislike heavy, poorly-drained land. Light ground can be improved by adding strawy manure, compost or anything that will increase the humus content. There should be no lack of potash which is needed for the colouring of the berries apart from the production of good firm wood and the keeping of the foliage in good condition. Leaf scorch, a condition in which the edges of the leaves turn brown is the result of potash shortage. An application of fish manure at 57 g (2 oz.) to the square metre (sq.yd.) applied in February or early March every four years, will keep the bushes in good order. Wood ashes are an excellent alternative or sulphate of potash at 57 g (2 oz.) to the square metre (sq.yd.) can be used.

A sunny situation suits the bushes but both frost pockets and windy situations should be avoided. November is an ideal month for planting, so long as the soil is workable, although the bushes can also be moved in February and early March. They are usually available at two or three years old. If you intend to train red currants the younger specimens will be the easiest to manage but the older ones will, of course, come into bearing sooner.

[30]

It is not difficult to train red currants into single, double or triple cordons and all of these shapes are useful for training against a wall or fence where they take up little room.

Where a number of red currants are being planted they should be spaced about 1.8 m (6 ft.) apart. This will give them plenty of room to develop and allow for the eight or nine strong branches each bush should have. Single stemmed cordons should be spaced 45 cm (18 in.) apart at an angle of 45°. Apart from being grown against fences or walls they can be trained on light trellis work and used for dividing the fruit garden without taking up a lot of room.

It is best to keep red currant bushes to one leg or clean stem of about 15 cm (6 in.) before allowing branches to form. All suckers and buds below this point should be removed. This also applies to double and triple cordons and to espalier-shaped specimens. Red currants will grow well on north walls where the fruit will ripen later thus extending the season of use.

With regard to pruning, ideally, the bushes should have four main stems coming from the 'leg'. If in the first year these are each cut back to within 8–10 cm (3–4 in.) of their base it will result in the development of shapely fruit-producing specimens.

When the bushes are dormant, prune these shoots back to half their length, and the side-shoots to within a couple of buds of their base. In the case of single cordons, the leader must be pruned back several centimetres each year and all the side shoots cut to one bud. This will result in fruiting spurs. Once cordons reach 2 m (6 ft.) or so high, it is best to prevent them growing taller. If not checked the lower spurs may become unproductive. Cordons must be fixed to strong supports to keep the main stem straight.

Red currants can be trained as espaliers, but need rather more care in pruning and training. They will normally have three or four tiers up to 30 cm (12 in.) apart formed by retaining one vertical leader, two equal and opposite side-shoots forming each tier. The main stem and the tiers or arms must be kept tied to supports. All buds forming on the main stem between the arms must be rubbed out and the shoots pruned back to the first bud annually.

It is an advantage to summer-prune trained red currants, the

{31}

side-shoots being cut back to five leaves but the leaders should be left untouched. The best time to summer-prune is when the berries are starting to colour. If done too early, unwanted secondary shoots may develop, if delayed too long, there will be no check to the stronger shoots which is one of the main objects of summer-pruning.

Instead of shortening the shoots by cutting them with a knife, some growers simply break off the side-shoots. This not only lets the sun and air into the centre of the bushes but induces fruit buds to form more freely at the base of the laterals.

Little is required in regard to general cultivation. Deep soil working should be avoided, since the roots of red currants are near the surface. An annual spring mulch of compost or strawy manure will do much good. If growth is slow, a dressing of a nitrogenous manure will usually speed development.

Some gardeners work in sulphate of ammonia at the rate of 14–28 g (½-1 oz.) to the square metre.

When gathering the fruit pick with the strig, taking care not to break the spurs, from which will come the next years crop.

3. *White Currants*

Although not grown on a wide scale these are cultivated in exactly the same way as red varieties. There are several named sorts all of which should be planted not less than 1.3 m (4 ft.) apart. The following are reliable.

White Dutch This forms a spreading bush which carries medium-sized bunches of berries.

Late White Grape Probably the best variety for general purposes. The finely flavoured juicy berries are splendid for dessert use, being produced on very long bunches.

White Transparent or *White Pearl,* mid-season bears a heavy crop of good-sized berries.

White Versailles is an early variety, producing long bunches of large good-flavoured fruit.

All white currants need careful handling at picking time and afterwards, for the berries can easily become bruised or crushed.

White currants should be grown on a 'leg' of 15–30 cm (9–12 in.) all buds being removed from the cuttings except four or five at the top. It is

[32]

advisable to make the cuttings 23–25 cm (9–10 in.) long and to bury them to a depth of about 15 cm (6 in.). If a quantity of cuttings are being rooted they should be placed 8 to 10 cm (3 or 4 in.) apart, with 60 cm (2 ft.) between rows. Subsequently, the young specimens must be pruned to make shapely bushes. To do this, always cut to an outward pointing bud and keep suckers removed.

Propagation is from hardwood cuttings. The best time for the job is in the early autumn when they usually root easily. One year-old shoots should be selected from strong healthy bushes.

Although some fruit is borne on young shoots much is carried on the spurs of old wood. Pruning consists of shortening by half the stems of newly planted bushes. In subsequent years the same procedure is followed. This will keep the bushes to the same height especially as the laterals should be shortened in summer.

Mulching with decayed manure is useful, particularly when the bushes are young, while top dressings of bonfire ash or sulphate of potash encourage firm growth.

CRANBERRY *(Vaccinium oxycoccus)*
This is another subject of which the culture might well be extended. This fruit has been grown in substantial quantities in Holland and North America for a long time and already investigations are being made into the possibilities of cranberry growing on a larger scale in this country.

While it is not yet certain whether commercial cultivation is practicable there is no reason why this subject should not be grown in gardens on a small scale. The cranberry plant is a trailing vine with upright branches of 15–20 cm (6–8 in.) high. It flowers in June and July when all danger of frost has passed, fruit being ready for harvesting from September onwards.

Cranberries have a shallow rooting system and therefore the soil depth need not be great. They do well in a few centimetres of peat over sand or clay. On the other hand peat does not appear to be essential. Although the soil should stay fairly moist throughout the year, it must not remain really wet for any period during the growing season, as poor drainage favours weeds and encourages pests and diseases.

With regard to propagation, cuttings form a ready means of increase

[33]

c

and they can consist of shoots 25–30 cm (10–12 in.) long taken from late April onwards. They will root easily in sandy, peaty soil. For small numbers, boxes may be used but in larger quantities cuttings can be inserted directly in rows in frames or in the open ground.

Growers often leave the cuttings untrimmed, and they seem able to root quite well if they are simply scattered on the surface and lightly covered with soil.

ELDER (*Sambucus nigra*)

This widely distributed shrub or small tree is not usually held in high esteem although it has for centuries been closely connected with legend and folk-lore. At one time it was believed to be unlucky to uproot elder trees growing near the house – and they were once often to be found close to cottage walls – since it was believed they acted as a protection against witches.

Apart from the fact that it was thought they brought luck, elder has at various times been noted for its healing powers. All parts of the tree are of value. The flowers are useful medicinally and for cosmetic purposes. When dried, the flowers contain various oils and mucilage being of use in increasing perspiration while they can act as a blood purifier and have been used successfully for the relief of asthma, colds and for the making of a general tonic, which is mildly astringent. Water from boiled flowers is used to cleanse the skin, while elder flower ointment is helpful in the case of chilblains, chaps and scalds.

The berries are also of value and have been used for the relief of laryngitis, sciatica and other rheumatic complaints. When lightly boiled or eaten with honey, they are quite tasty, as is elderberry jam which needs only a little sugar and lemon juice to make it first class. Elderberry wine is always worth making and drinking. The leaves are said to keep away flies if they are bruised.

The elder is of simple cultivation and although seedlings often appear in gardens it is best to obtain the true *Sambucus nigra*. The heavily scented white or creamy flowers appear in June and July, being produced in flat umbel-like clusters as much as 12–20 cm (5–8 in.) across. They are followed by shiny blackish-violet berries. Culture is not difficult, since almost any soil which does not dry out is suitable. A sunny situation is best. Pruning can be done during the dormant season. Propagation is simply by cuttings of basal shoots or by root division.

FIG (*Ficus carica*)

For most of us the mention of figs immediately brings to mind those tightly packed boxes or blocks of dried fruit so much in demand at Christmas time. Such figs, of course, come from the East, for they are natives of Syria and surrounding countries.

Since climatic conditions in those parts are so congenial it will rapidly be realized that figs are not suitable for growing in the open ground in all parts of the country. Certainly a few may be found developing fairly happily against sheltered south-facing walls, but it is in the glass-house that they give of their best. Although not grown commercially in great quantities, there is no reason why an attempt should not be made to cultivate figs, for with a few cultural details attended to, they are well worth the effort.

Young plants in small pots are offered by several of our leading nursery-men and although there is usually a choice of varieties, *Brown Turkey* is perhaps the most reliable, followed by *Brunswick*. The former has brownish-red fruits with red flesh, and is very fertile, while Brunswick ripens rather later, is larger, and of a green colour with white flesh. Both are strong growing and can usually be relied upon to crop well. *White Marseille* is a very early large pear-shaped variety with pale green skin and sweet red fruit.

The end of March or during April are good times to transfer figs from the pots in which they are grown to the glasshouse border, or in some instances they will grow happily when they are moved into bigger receptacles.

The site in the greenhouse should be well prepared and dug to a depth of 60 cm (2 ft.) or so, being provided with plenty of drainage material and it is well worth putting in a layer of brickbats, stones, mortar, rubble, etc. A good loamy soil is suitable while the addition of really old decayed horse or stable manure will prove helpful. Bone meal at the rate of 85–113 g (3–4 oz.) to the square metre worked well into the compost will provide additional feeding material over a long period.

Fruit is produced on new season's growth and it has been found that if

[35]

as the plants develop they are trained into a more-or-less fan shape they will yield well. In fact it is noticeable that the greatest amount of the best fruit is usually carried on the lower branches so that it is a practice of some growers to encourage the branches to develop fairly near the ground, or to pull them into that position. On this system some kind of support with stakes or wire will be necessary, but even with bush specimens, the branches can be trained so that they are encouraged to grow rather horizontally.

Once established the fruit begins to ripen towards the end of May and develops on the new shoots which are produced on the previous season's stems which have been pruned back. Further fruit develops intermittently during the summer.

Pruning is important both to keep the trees in shape and to provide a regular supply of new shoots which will bear well. Often only very little cutting is necessary this being done during July and August. Although good drainage is essential, figs must have plenty of moisture throughout the growing season.

A moist atmosphere during the summer is also advisable and can be secured by frequent overhead sprayings of clear water, which at the same time, will prevent red spider from being troublesome. When this pest does gain a hold it will spoil the appearance of the fruit. Occasional applications of liquid manure are helpful and if the temperature can be kept to about 15°C. (60°F.) it will suit figs admirably although naturally the thermometer will rise higher during spells of strong sunshine.

Outdoors figs can be grown against walls with a sunny aspect. The best method of training is the fan system. This simply implies spreading out the shoots and securing them in position. Never crowd the growths since only with sufficient room, sunlight and warmth, will a crop mature. Avoid rich heavy soils for these lead to rank leafy growth with little fruit. Firm, well-ripened wood is needed for crop bearing.

If the trees are to fruit well it is essential that the root system is restricted. The bed should be dug out about 60 cm (2 ft.) deep and the bottom of the hole filled with bricks or stone slabs. This will allow for drainage and prevent tap-root formation. However a fig is planted, it is essential to bear in mind that fruitfulness is dependant on a restricted root system.

The fig is unique in the way it fruits for a fruiting branch will usually carry quite large figs on its lower portion, followed by very small fruits. At the top of the same stems there are normally tiny embryo fruits no larger than peas. The latter are the crop for the next season. It is quite usual to remove the second-sized fruit for it is rarely that this crop has time to ripen at the end of the summer.

To have their full flavour, figs must ripen on the trees, although there are several, often old-fashioned, ways of inducing earlier ripening. One of these is to dip a needle in olive oil and push it into the eye of the fig.

Propagation can be done by making cuttings in September, by layering or taking out suckers in autumn.

In the event of prolonged severe weather, figs can be protected by spreading litter around the tree base and fixing straw over the branches.

GOOSEBERRY

The gooseberry has had a chequered career, for sometimes it has been in great favour, while on other occasions it seems to have been lightly esteemed. Probably, the greatest influences on the development of this truly English fruit, were the Gooseberry Competitions held in the Midlands. The test of merit was weight, and in spite of the smoke and other disadvantages of industrial towns, many marvellous berries were produced.

A hundred or more years ago, show gooseberries were very fashionable, in fact, some firms listed more than a hundred varieties for exhibition and general purposes. Today, few firms offer more than a dozen varieties, most only six or seven sorts.

Particularly in Lancashire, gooseberry fanciers were very keen. An old record shows that one variety, oddly enough named *London,* secured nearly 360 awards at shows during 1867. Then the names of the gooseberry seedlings of those days seemed to reflect the political history of earlier years, the titles of some popular sorts being of politicians, including Lords Brougham and Eldon. Royalty was not overlooked in these names, and there was *Queen Caroline, Prince Regent* and the *Princess Royal.*

Undoubtedly this great interest in gooseberries, led to the increase in size, and probably flavour too. It does seem, however, that because of the

[37]

un-exciting origin of the gooseberry, it has never been valued as it should be, being regarded as a substitute when other fruits were not available.

Anyone who has tasted some of the better varieties, will know that the gooseberry has a distinct flavour, and if it were to come to us as an imported fruit, it would be much more highly valued.

When the fruit is picked prematurely, the full flavour is not there, and undoubtedly many people judge gooseberries on the unripe samples so often to be found in the shop and market. Then there are those who object to hairy fruits, but many of these are of superb flavour.

The colour of the berries also seems to have some influence on demand, and the fruit is sometimes judged on its colour without it being sampled. Very often the yellow varieties are considered best-flavoured. Of these, *Yellow Rough* or *Early Sulphur,* although hairy, and not of the largest size, are first class. For bigger fruit, *Criterion, Catherina* and *Gunner* are outstanding. As to smooth-skinned varieties, *Leveller* and *Leader* are superb.

Red varieties need to be eaten for dessert just at the right moment. Although not readily available at the present, and not amongst the largest sorts, *Ironmonger* and *Red Champagne,* both hairy, are delightful. For a larger red, the still popular *Whinham's Industry* is a variety difficult to beat for flavour.

There are few so-called white gooseberries, grown at the present time. Some of these certainly have many good qualities. *Mitre, White Swan* and *Snowdrops,* apparently non-existent today, are all of excellent flavour, and are hairy to some degree. As to the smooth whites, *Transparent,* though scarce, is excellent, while *Careless* probably now the most grown white sort, should not be overlooked.

Green varieties are among the finest of all gooseberries, so long as they are gathered and eaten at the right time. Of these, the delicious hairy *Glenton Green* and *Green Gascoigne* seem to have gone out of cultivation, but are worth searching for. The same is true of *Ocean,* which is a large, smooth-skinned sort. *Langley Gage* and *Lancer* provide a succession.

While much fruit is often eaten straight from the bushes, the flavour is brought out best when the berries have been picked and kept in the warm for a few hours before being eaten.

While the thinning of gooseberries is not an essential part of their culture, it should be done if the very largest and finest berries are to be gathered from such sorts as Langley Gage and Leveller. In most cases the thinnings can be used for cooking.

While all gooseberries can be cooked, some of the real dessert varieties, such as Leveller, are far better eaten raw and lose some of their good flavour when cooked. Culinary sorts, such as *May Duke,* while first class for pies, tarts and jams, are only of moderate quality when used for dessert.

Trained trees seem to produce the largest and best fruit, probably because the number of berries is smaller. There is no point in leaving fruit on the bushes until it bursts.

It is advisable to prune the bushes regularly in order to keep them shapely. The reduction of growths aids the development of really fine quality fruit of good flavour.

The gooseberry is not without its pests but if these are dealt with at an early stage they should not present any great problem. Aphides or greenfly are probably most persistent. Bushes can usually be kept cleared of these if they are given a tar oil wash in December. A 1.13 l (1 qt.) of oil being mixed with 22.7 l (5 gal.) of water is a first class way of keeping down aphides.

Gooseberry Sawfly Caterpillars can be killed by spraying liquid derris. If this is done first in May, and then in June, with a third spraying towards the end of August, it should give a complete control. Attacking both currants and gooseberries, the *Currant Clear Wing Caterpillar* is a pest which tunnels up the interior of the branches, causing them to become distorted and often to die. So far, there is no known cure for this pest.

The *Magpie Moth,* so called because of its black and white caterpillars which appear during August, can be effectively controlled by applying derris in liquid form.

American gooseberry mildew is very well known, and causes the leaves to be covered with a white felt-like substance which eventually turns a dirty brown colour. The berries too, are frequently attacked and spoiled. The main reason for growing gooseberries on a 'leg' or short stem, is to keep the branches from the soil. They will then be less likely to attacks by this form of mildew.

Many growers find it an advantage to mulch the ground around the bushes with straw, for this keeps the leaves from contacting the earth. Pruning should be done carefully in order to allow plenty of sun, light and air to all branches. The bushes should not be planted too closely together or in the shade of trees.

As a means of controlling this form of mildew, it is a good plan to mix 454 g (1 lb) of washing soda and 113 g (¼ lb) of soft soap with 22.7 l (5 gal.) of water and to spray this over the bushes, taking care to reach the undersides of the leaves.

If gooseberries are grown under healthy conditions and the soil is not deficient in potash, there is little fear that they will be seriously affected by disease of any kind.

GRAPE VINE *(Vitis vinifera)*

There is plenty of evidence to show that grape-vines have been grown for centuries. Certainly they were a crop greatly valued by the ancient Israelites who esteemed them for their health-promoting qualities. The Romans brought them to Britain and no doubt to other countries too. Good wine was once produced in several English counties including Gloucestershire, Worcester and Essex and it is difficult to understand why production ceased.

It may have been at least partly due to the dissolution of the monasteries, for at these establishments the cultivation of vines was regularly practised. Gradually it seems, the idea became widespread that grapes could be grown successfully only in heated greenhouses. Whatever the cause, the British seemed to have accepted the idea that grapes needed hothouse culture. This may have been the propaganda of the French and Italians, since these people have built up a big export business sending extremely large quantities of wine to Britain and many other countries.

During the last thirty years there has been a remarkable revival in grape growing outdoors as well as under glass and many people have learned the skills of producing a good crop and making acceptable wine. It is largely due to the work of the Viticultural Research Station at Oxted, Surrey, under the direction of Mr Barrington Brock, that so much more is now known about the successful growing of grapes outdoors.

Dealing first with greenhouse cultivation, ideally the site should be one which drains naturally and where there is a good depth of light calcareous loam. Much can be done to provide suitable rooting conditions. It has long been the practice of gardeners to plant their vines on an outside border and to work the rods through holes in the wall and then to train the rods on wires, in the usual manner inside the greenhouse. When this is done drainage must be good, for vines will not tòlerate stagnant moisture round their roots. The one disadvantage in planting outside is that in very wet weather during the fruit-ripening period, the fruit may split.

When planting inside the greenhouse some gardeners make sure they have complete control of moisture by making a brick-lined planting hole. This should be about 1 m (3 ft.) deep at the back sloping to 75 cm (2½ ft.) at the front in order to prevent water logged roots. Width of the site will depend on the size of the house, but should certainly not be less than 1½ m (4½ ft.) Brickbats should be placed at the bottom of the hole before filling it with good rich loam, decayed manure and leaf mould with a good sprinkling of bone meal.

Vines should be transplanted while dormant. For preference, the period of late November to the end of January is best avoided, and it is advisable to buy pot-grown plants. These need to be taken out carefully making sure not to damage the rods. Some gardeners prefer to shake the soil from the roots believing that this ensures the plants are loosened from the pot shape into which they have been confined. Spread the roots evenly covering them gently with about 10 cm (4 in.) of soil and making it firm. Then give a thorough soaking of water which should have the chill taken off.

If growing more than one vine at least 2 m (6 ft.) should be allowed between them, while individual rods should not be spaced closer than 90 cm (3 ft.)

Vines are natural climbers having tendrils with which to grasp anything they can find for support. They are normally vigorous growers with many branches and leaves. Various methods of training are adopted when cultivating vines under glass. The training starts the first summer after planting. By then the rod and new growth will be supported by a cane, pushed in the soil about 15 cm (6 in.) deep. The top of the cane should reach just past the first horizontal strand of wire to which it can be tied. Next a 2.7–3 m (9–10 ft.) bamboo cane must be fixed to the top of the cane supporting the vine, and also to the first strand of wire. As growth proceeds the young leading shoot should be tied to the cane as it grows towards the top wire in the roof.

The side-shoots should be kept rubbed out from the axils of the leaves until the last leaf from the wire is reached. From this point allow the growths or laterals to make two or three leaves before the little shoots are pinched out.

Established vines in full growth will need looking over twice weekly, so that unwanted shoots can be removed and the plant's energy is not wasted. Stop the leaders when they reach the third wire from the top. Not only is this necessary because the shoots have reached the limit of their space but the fruit which forms on the top laterals can be supported on these highest wires.

Keep the tendrils removed for if left they will grasp the wires, leaves and laterals and become a general nuisance. As a result of stopping the laterals they too, will almost certainly produce further shoots. These are known as sub-laterals and they in turn, should be pinched back at the first leaf. It is quite a good plan after the rod has been stopped, to allow some of the sub-laterals to grow. This not only helps the rod to become stronger but keeps the roots in action by reason of the necessity of supplying nourishment to the new growths.

As autumn approaches, more ventilation can be allowed. This helps the maturing of the vines. The rod should be a nice brown shade, an indication that it has ripened and is in good condition for producing a crop the next year. Pruning can be started in November once the vine is dormant. If left until after the middle of December the cuts are liable to bleed badly and loss of sap leads to a weakening of the vine.

Although it sometimes appears to be complicated, pruning is not at all difficult. The thickish lateral buds that form in the axil of each primary leaf should be cut off at the end of the first growing season. If growth has not been good and the rod seems unable to make real progress it is advisable to cut it back to within three strong buds from ground level. Such action will stimulate good growth the following year.

In subsequent years when the vine has reached its allotted space, each lateral is cut back to two, sometimes one strong bud from which further laterals will be produced the following season. This means that there is a gradual lengthening of the spurs as a result of the regular cutting back of the laterals.

There are several other ways of pruning, one, known as the 'new rod' system which eventually means the cutting out of the old central leader and replacing it by two laterals from the lower spurs. This seems well worthwhile when a vine has begun to lose some of its vigour and cropping power owing to age.

The tying of the laterals is another important job and needs to be done with care or the shoots will snap off. Wide raffia is the best material to use and often it is not possible to complete the job at one time for fear of the shoot breaking. In such cases it is best to go carefully and to do the job in stages.

Top dressing can do a lot of good. First very carefully remove the surface soil around the vine, making sure not to damage the fibrous shallow roots. Then, top dress with a mixture of three parts good loam and one part each rotted stable manure and bonfire ash. A good dusting of lime and bone meal make valuable additions.

Where heat is available it is possible to start vines into growth towards the end of November. This is necessary only where grapes are wanted in April and May. Very often however, the vines are not started until early March. This means that fruit will be ready for gathering from August onwards. Early maturing grapes such as the popular *Black Hamburgh* and *Madresfield Court* can usually be cut within five months of being started, but the majority of varieties need six months to mature.

Some greenhouse vines do not set heavy crops, without the help of artificial pollination. *Muscat of Alexandria* is one of these. If *Black Hamburgh* or *Alicante* are grown in the same house as the Muscat of Alexandria it will be easy to go from flower to flower with a camel hair brush and distribute pollen from fertilization.

Once the fruit has set the berries develop quickly and some thinning out will be necessary. No rod should be allowed to carry more than ten to twelve bunches for overcropping can prove harmful. Having retained the right number of bunches the next step is to thin out the berries. This can be done best with specially pointed vine scissors. The shape of the

[43]

bunches varies according to the variety being grown, some having much broader shoulders than others. Some varieties have very short footstalks which makes it difficult to thin the berries if the operation is delayed. Particularly with large bunches, it is helpful to tie out the shoulders, especially if grapes are needed for exhibition. When thinning the bunches, the berries retained should not be touched by the hands or anything else.

Once the main thinning has been done, it is wise to look at the bunches from time to time, not only to remove odd berries as necessary, but also to remove the seedless berries which will not mature properly. When the bunches begin to enlarge the vines can be helped by liquid feeds. There are many brands which if used as instructed can be most helpful; a dilution of dried blood as well as a weak solution of nitrate of potash will do good. Some growers rely on a top dressing and a spring mulch of manure to keep the vines in full production.

As soon as the berries begin to colour, ventilation should be increased without allowing draughts. One problem in giving more air is that birds may be tempted to attack the fruit. They can be stopped by covering the vents with perforated zinc which, incidentally, will also keep out wasps. It is unwise to gather the bunches before the berries are mature for then the sugars have not completely changed and the berries are still acid.

Ripe grapes will keep in good condition for quite a long time if treated properly. There are many ways of keeping them but the best is to erect a 'bottle rack'. This is made by fixing suitable wooden 'arms' to a square of wood several feet high. These arms support bottles of water at an angle of about $45°$. The cut stems holding the bunches of grapes are put in the neck of the bottle until they reach the water which will keep the berries in good condition for a long time. A few lumps of charcoal should be placed in the bottle before the water is put in.

One great advantage of growing grape-vines in large pots is that the development of the plant is under complete control. There is no question of it having to be trained up the side of the house and on to the rafters. When planted in the border in the usual way this is what has to happen and the foliage cuts off much light from the plants below. This means that the range of other plants that can be grown is very limited.

There are quite a number of varieties which respond really well to pot culture. These include Black Hamburgh which is one of the best known of all grapes. It is robust growing and free bearing, the roundish berries having a bluish-black skin with a pronounced bloom. When the bunches are well thinned, the berries are often over an inch in diameter. Like other thin-skinned varieties, its flavour is at its best when the berries are just ripe. It does not lend itself to late keeping.

Royal Muscadine is also good for pot culture. The smallish round berries are greenish-yellow, becoming a bright cinnamon-russet colour when exposed to bright sunlight. It is then that the flavour is at its best.

To start growing grapes in pots, you should get a one year-old plant from a specialist grower. It will come to you in a 12–15 cm (5–6 in.) pot, in the autumn. It should be moved to a 30 cm (12 in.) pot after it has been in the greenhouse for some weeks. The John Innes Compost No. 3 is suitable or you can make a soil mixture on the following lines: to five parts of good fibrous loam, add one part each, well-decayed manure (preferably horse) and old mortar rubble, ½ part coarse bone meal and a sprinkling of wood ash. Failing the latter, seaweed fertilizer or sulphate of potash can be used. Make sure that the pots are well crocked before putting in the compost.

The vine must be trained in the form of a hoop. Insert two 1.3 m (4 ft.) canes, one on each side of the pot and join their tops by another cane tied horizontally. As the vine grows, it is trained up one cane, across the top and down the other side. Laterals will, of course, develop at intervals and these must be restricted or rubbed out so that there is 30 cm (12 in.) between those that are left.

Each of the shoots that are allowed to develop should be stopped, or have its growing point pinched out at the second leaf beyond the embryo bunch of grapes. Only one bunch of fruit should be allowed on each lateral and it is unwise to let a pot vine carry more than 6 or 7 bunches in one year.

After fruiting is over, the vine can be plunged in the open ground, just as it is, in the pot. Choose a sunny situation to help the 'wood' to ripen. It can remain there until the autumn, when it can be moved to the greenhouse. Before doing so, carefully take out the top 8 cm (3 in.) of compost from the pot and replace it with good rich compost.

Obviously, the time of starting the pot vine in the house will affect the

[45]

time of ripening. Started in a warm house in November or December, fruit should be ready for cutting in April or May respectively. In a cool house, the fruit will ripen in early July. If there is no heat available grapes will be ripe from August onwards.

Pruning must be carried out while the vine is dormant. This entails shortening the main stem by cutting away half the previous season's growth and cutting back the side-shoots or laterals to two buds.

It is not really worth keeping a pot vine after the third year. It can be replaced by a fresh plant from a nurseryman or, if you have a warm greenhouse it will not be difficult to raise a new plant by rooting an 'eye' from one of the strong laterals of the vine which has fruited. If one or two new plants are propagated annually, there will always be a supply of young specimens available which means that there will not be a break in fruiting.

Propagation can be done in January or February. There are various methods, including layering, cuttings and the taking of 'eyes'. The latter is the most satisfactory. It is done by saving well-ripened laterals when pruning is done in November or December. These should have really good plump buds and should be buried to half their depth out of doors. Towards the end of February, prepare some 8 cm (3 in.) pots of sandy, peaty loam and then bring in the laterals from the open ground.

Cut these into lengths so that each one is about 5 cm (2 in.) long, with a plump bud in the centre. Press one of these pieces into each pot of compost without burying the bud. Ideally, the pot should then be plunged into a propagating frame and with bottom heat, growth will be rapid. Many of us, however, cannot do this and the pots can be placed in the warmest part of the greenhouse, where growth though slower, is normally good. Subsequently, the rooted 'eyes' will need moving first to 13 cm (5 in.) and then to larger size pots.

It is also possible to root vine 'eyes' in pieces of turf into which they should be securely pegged to encourage quick growth.

Diseases

Mildew is one of the diseases the vine grower is almost certain to encounter. It is of fungal origin and unless dealt with in its earliest stages, it can become a really serious menace both under glass and in the open.

It affects leaves and flowers, the network of fungus filaments appearing as a white powdering. Under glass much can be done to combat this trouble by avoiding low, damp temperatures and draughts. Broken panes of glass and badly fitting ventilators should therefore be put right. Occasional sprayings with Benlate will usually prevent most forms of mildew from gaining a hold. Alternatively dustings of fine yellow sulphur if applied early will be effective especially if congenial growing conditions are maintained. Better perhaps than an ordinary dusting is the use of a sulphur vaporizer. Two applications with two or three days between will usually be sufficient. Once this happens it is a good plan to give further occasional dustings as a precaution against future attacks.

Downy mildew is a more serious disease but fortunately, comparatively rare. It is believed to have been introduced from the United States over ninety years ago. If it gains a hold both leaves and fruit cease to grow. Control of the disease is effected through the use of a fungicide with a copper sulphate base.

Rust is another possibility. This is not actually a disease but the result of some faulty conditions. Draughts caused by faulty ventilation, a hot dry atmosphere, or physical contact are all possible causes. If these conditions are avoided rust should not occur.

Scalding is the result of moisture condensing on the berries which are slower in warming than the atmosphere. This means that ventilation plays a big part in keeping the berries from becoming spoiled. Excepting in really warm houses, the atmosphere is liable to become quite cool in the early morning. Once the sun becomes powerful the temperature rises rapidly unless ventilation is given. It is this sudden rise in heat which can lead to scalding. The remedy is obvious.

Shanking is a term applied by grape growers when the footstalks of berries dry up before they are ripe. This may be while they are green or more often as they begin to colour. The dark coloured varieties remain a greenish-red shade and become useless.

This disorder may arise if the vine roots remain waterlogged or very dry for any length of time. Sometimes with fairly old specimens, it is an indication that the roots have worked their way into unfavourable conditions. The soil may have become sour and airless, even though it was originally prepared with care.

Where the vines are not particularly old a lot can be done to overcome the possibility of shanking by carefully removing some of the soil, replacing it with fresh well-drained rich compost.

Growing Grapes Outdoors

There is now a distinct interest in the growing of grapes for wine purposes. It is not only amateurs who are taking it up with a view to making wine for their own purposes, but there is a movement towards wider growing on a commercial or at least semi-commercial scale.

There was a time when the wine industry flourished in this country, but it is a very long time since it ceased to operate. It is a little difficult to know why this should be. It is not altogether because of an adverse climate, for neither weather or soil are altogether responsible for the prevention of growing grapes for wine, or dessert fruit, in the southern counties of England.

It is true that grapes do not always ripen well out of doors but this is more a problem for those who grow grapes for dessert purposes rather than for wine. There are so many varieties of grape-vines for growing out of doors that it is possible by choosing an early maturing variety or by covering the plants with cloches or similar glass structures to secure good bunches which if subsequently cut and hung in the greenhouse will gradually ripen.

Even so it is better to let the grapes ripen on the vines. Situation is important and it would be unwise to attempt to grow vines in frost pockets or low-lying districts. Grapes will grow on a wide range of soil although it does seem that those of a fairly light gravelly nature are best. Free-draining soil means that there is not likely to be waterlogged or sour root conditions.

Vines certainly need sunshine, but warmth is equally important and very often although there may not always be the amount of sun we would desire, the warmth can be provided by using the shelter of a south-facing wall or a thick hedge which gives protection from spring and summer winds. Whilst providing these it is essential not to create a frost pocket.

Since light gravelly soils do suit vines, it will be obvious that they will need to be enriched in order to provide the nourishment the vines will

[48]

require as they develop. Decayed manure and other humus-forming material will be specially beneficial. For the first two or three years after planting little or no manuring will be necessary for, during that period, the vines need to build up a framework of wood and the accent is not then on cropping.

After that more decayed farmyard manure and other organic fertilizers should be worked in. In established vineyards the aim should be to give a good manuring every third year or so and during these periods dressings of phosphates or potash fertilizers will prove beneficial. Digging in surface weeds during the autumn will help to increase the humus content of the soil which is most important if there is to be a free root system so necessary for the production of good bunches.

Planting distances for outdoor vines will depend on the system on which they are to be grown. It is usual and satisfactory to allow 1.2–1.35 m (4–4½ ft.) apart each way. When planting the roots should be spread out fully and evenly, and they should be about 10 cm (4 in.) below surface level. Plant firmly, making sure that the roots are in close contact with the soil. After planting, rake over the ground and give a good dressing of bone meal, lightly working it in. One-year vines are the best for transplanting, the ideal time being towards the end of October while the soil is still warm and easily workable.

Pruning is important and must be done regularly. Bear in mind that the fruit is borne on new wood, which means that the plants will increase in girth and not height. The object of severe pruning is the production of new wood, although this may have to be thinned, the berries seem to ripen better nearer the ground. January is a good time for pruning while the wood is dormant. If, however, the weather happens to be bad early in the year pruning should be delayed so long as the rods remain dormant.

It is not easy to be dictatorial about pruning since there are various methods or systems on which the vines can be trained, for instance there is the guyot system, in which the vine is allowed to grow naturally for two seasons, there should then be two long rods with a number of laterals. Cut back all the side-shoots to one strong bud from the base, any weak canes need only be cut back to within two buds. Then the rods are bent round and tied into a half circle. Some growers retain only one rod, others leave two, both of which are trained into the half or full circle.

[49]

D

The goblet system aims at producing an open bush-like shape. Here again pruning is important and should be done in January. Cut out all growths excepting the main rod, which should be allowed to develop naturally. The following year cut back this rod to within three buds of the base and these three buds should be allowed to develop and the young growth be tied to supports, being spaced to form a goblet shape. The following year cut back each of these rods, to within two buds of the base, so that the goblet then has six rods. This is followed by continued careful pruning, although no vines should be allowed to retain more than nine shoots. Vines can also be trained as cordons and espaliers when they will fruit heavily if planted against a warm wall.

Varieties for outdoor growing

Chasselas Ciolat An attractive cut-leaved variety. First class for wall culture. The greenish-white berries are sometimes slow in ripening.

Chasselas Rose A good grape variety with pinkish ornamental berries. Excellent for walls and grows well under tall frames.

Ganay Hative des Vosges A heavy cropper, the black berries though rather small being of good flavour. This variety is much used for wine.

Muscat de Saumur An early muscat with large bunches of medium-sized golden berries.

Muscat Hamburgh Although useful for greenhouses it also succeeds on warm walls and is excellent for cloches and frames where the black berries ripen well.

Noir Hatif de Marseille A highly recommended dessert grape, the black berries being produced in large clusters.

Pirovano 14 Useful for dessert and wine, the black grapes being freely produced.

Precoce de Malingre A good cropping early variety, the small oval yellow grapes being of fine flavour.

Riesling Sylvaner A mid-season reliable variety, the golden grapes being good for eating or for making a fine Hock-type wine.

Royal Muscadine (Chasselas or *Golden Muscadine)* Of excellent size and good flavour the thin-skinned greenish berries ripening well in the open and under cloches.

White Frontignan Another heavy cropping variety with medium-sized grapes of good flavour.

[50]

Wrotham Pinot This is believed to be one of the varieties grown centuries ago. Although not a heavy cropper, the small black grapes make a good Burgundy-type wine.

There are a number of so-called American varieties which are useful for wines. Of those usually available from British nurserymen the following are worth growing.

Brandt Hardy and vigorous growing and useful for covering trellis work. The smallish black berries are good tasting.

Concord is another hardy variety, the medium-sized black berries making good red wine. It does best on a lime-free soil.

Strawberry This has thin-skinned fruit with a trace of strawberry flavour. A good cropper, the ornamental glossy pink berries with a slight strawberry fragrance being freely produced in small bunches. Will grow well against a wall if given some support. Only the ripened shoots survive severe frosts but new growth is made each spring.

Propagation

Outdoor grape-vines can be propagated by various means such as eyes, cuttings, layers, grafting by approach and sometimes by budding. Vines can also be raised from seeds but the resultant plants rarely ever bear fruit which even approaches anything like that of the best named varieties. As with other forms of sowing it is just possible that by sowing seed from two selected parents one might be fortunate enough to raise a seedling superior to either but the chances are extremely slight.

The easiest method of propagation is undoubtedly from eyes or single buds which are cut from well-ripened wood including prunings and which form the centre of a piece of stem about 5 cm (2 in.) long. For this one needs to have a heated house for starting off the eyes towards the end of February.

Normally, vines are pruned in November or December and at that time well-ripened laterals can be selected and tied in bundles first being labelled and then buried to half their depth in soil out of doors. Obviously only those laterals which are vigorous and have good plump buds are worth considering for propagation.

From the middle of February onwards the plan should be to make up 8 cm (3 in.) pots of sharp sand and loam, one pot for each eye. Better still if fibrous turf is available this can be cut up into pieces about 15 cm (6 in.) long and 8 cm (3 in.) wide and deep using one of these pieces for each eye. These pieces of turf can be kept in seed trays with their grass side downwards. Whether pots of soil or turf are used the bud is prepared in the same way. To do this a thin boat-shaped strip about 25 mm (1 in.) long is cut from the underside of the wood from which the bud arises although some growers simply cut the pieces without shaping them.

This bud is then laid horizontally with sufficient soil covering to leave just the tip showing. Stand the pots of turf in a warm propagating house, keeping the soil just moist and the buds slightly damp to encourage them to start into growth. Alternatively, a propagating frame may be used and where a bottom heat of 20°C. (70°F.) is available in a greenhouse having a temperature of 12°–15°C. (55°–60°F.) this will induce early growth. It is often necessary to start buds under less congenial conditions and as a rule there is no difficulty in getting them to grow although development will be slower.

Where it is not possible to raise vines by eyes, it can be done by cuttings. Materials used for these must be vigorous, first-year laterals with good plump buds. The cuttings are secured and prepared at the time of pruning the vines, each cutting having three buds which means that a clean cut must be made immediately above the top bud and again below the bottom one. The middle and bottom buds are removed leaving the top plump one.

One prepared cutting should be inserted in each pot under a cold frame, cloche or similar glass protection. For preference use deep pots to give room for root development. A sandy loam is very suitable to use as a rooting medium. While the soil in the pots must not become dry at any time, it would be fatal for it to become waterlogged. If the actual pots can be plunged in weathered coke ash or something similar this will ensure that the compost does not dry out.

Towards the end of February it is advisable to bring the pots into the cool or warm greenhouse and once it is seen that the buds are beginning to swell, they should be placed in full light fairly near to the glass in order to develop their leaves.

When the cuttings have produced three or four leaves by which time they will also have made a good root system, they should be potted singly. Keep them in a close, moist atmosphere for a week or so after they have been moved. This will prevent the leaves from becoming limp through root disturbance and will also ensure there is a quick recovery. As a rule it is not less than three years from the time vine cuttings are rooted until they fruit.

Another much less common way of propagating vines is by layering. This is done by securing a young rod from the lowest spur on a vigorous, well-established vine. Ideally, the cane to be layered should be 3–3.6 m (10–12 ft.) or more long, fairly thick and of good rich brown colour, showing that it is mature.

This cane can be shortened, and the laterals removed. Then the rod is passed through the hole in the bottom of a 23–25 cm (9–10 in.) plant pot which is placed on the staging or other suitable firm place. Then make an incision with a sharp knife immediately below a joint which is fairly near the bottom of the pot. Make the cut about half-way through the stem then bind damp peat round the cut rod in order to encourage root formation.

Then fill the pot with good sandy loam keeping it uniformly moist. This rod will, if treated normally, produce bunches of grapes the same year. After they have been gathered, the rod should be severed at the bottom of the pot, but it must be done with great care in order to avoid bleeding.

Subsequently, this separate vine can be trained up in the usual way. It is a good idea to reduce some of the leaves after the rod has been severed, in order to check undue transpiration. Fairly close shady conditions should be provided for a time, after the rod has been severed from the parent.

Inarching or grafting by approach, is a method of propagation used for a number of ornamental subjects and it can be employed successfully on vines, although not often practised. It is useful if one wishes to test the quality of seedlings or new varieties in the shortest possible time.

For this purpose the plant to be inarched should be cut back hard in winter to induce a strong new rod to develop. The vine to be used as the stock or root portion, should be encouraged to develop, a strong lateral from the lowest spur. Once the stock and scion roots are a year old, both pots are placed close together. When the vines are in flower an upward cut is made on the scion and a downward one on the stock. Then fit them together in the normal whip-and-tongue grafting manner and bind with wide raffia. The grafting binding should be examined frequently so that the raffia can be loosened as necessary. It is usually three months before the union is strong enough to be unbound but it is advisable to make sure that the join is really firm before removing the raffia.

Varieties

Among the best that have been grown for many years, the following are first class.

Alicante The large oval black berries are freely produced although the flavour is not as rich as many others.

Black Hamburgh Probably the best known of all. The large juicy berries are sweet-flavoured with tender flesh.

Buckland Sweetwater Bright green berries with thin skin showing an amber tinge.

Foster's Seedling A heavy cropping early variety for both unheated and warm greenhouse. The greenish-yellow berries are of pleasing flavour.

Gros Colmar The rich reddish-purple berries are sweet and juicy.

Lady Downe's Seedling A late variety; having firm purplish-black berries with a sweet rich flavour.

Madresfield Court An early muscat, freely producing its tender juicy rich-flavoured berries.

Mrs Pearson The round whitish-amber berries turn pink when ripe.

Muscat of Alexandria Inclined to be a shy setter. The large oval berries are pale amber with a sweet, rich muscat flavour.

Reine Olga is free cropping with medium-sized rose-pink grapes.

Royal Muscadine Sometimes catalogued as *Chasselas de Fountainbleau*, the smallish golden-yellow berries become a cinnamon shade when exposed to the sun. An old variety, it does well in a sheltered position outdoors and in the cold greenhouse.

GUAVA *(Psidium guava)*

Sometimes known as the strawberry bush this subject is widely cultivated in the Tropics and is not difficult to grow in the cool greenhouse, in a temperature of at least 10°C. (50°F.), although it is

[54]

rarely seen in Britain outside Botanic Gardens. In Brazil and other tropical areas guavas grow at least 5 m (15 ft.) high but in more temperate places they are much smaller. The white flowers appear in summer being followed by yellow almost globose-shaped fruit which is high in vitamin C content. It is from this species that the well known (usually imported) guava jelly is produced. *Psidium cattleianum,* the strawberry guava has purplish-red fruit.

They can be grown in pots of fibrous loam, silver sand and decayed manure and do well when trained against the back wall of the greenhouse, while they are quite happy when cultivated in the vinery. Plenty of water in the growing season with feeds of liquid manure from the time the berries set until they ripen should lead to many juicy fruits.

Propagation is by seed or cuttings of firm young shoots inserted in a warm propagating frame in spring while air layering is not difficult.

HUCKLEBERRIES

1. *Garden Huckleberry (Solanum nigrum guinnse)*

When first exhibited at a Royal Horticultural Society Show in 1958, they caused much interest. They are quite different from the shrubby huckleberry and they are in fact annuals raised from seed in the usual way.

Sowing is done in cold frames or under cloches early in the year, when all danger of spring frosts has past. The seedlings should be set out in double rows about 38 cm (15 in.) apart with the same distance between rows. They usually make nice bushy plants up to a metre (3 ft.) high, although sometimes, particularly if planted too close together, they become somewhat drawn and will grow considerably taller.

Nothing special is required in the way of cultivation, beyond keeping down the weeds. Staking is not needed and there are no specific pests. Fruiting usually begins about mid-September, and will go on until frosts arrive. Although seed can be sown in the open ground, it does mean that fruiting is later and with early frosts, the season will be short.

Care must be taken to see that the ordinary weed *Solanum nigrum,* does not become mixed with the cultivated plant, for these could be harmful to humans and animals. Although the fruit of garden huckleberries is unpleasant if eaten raw, when cooked, it has a most attractive flavour and huckleberry pie is appreciated by many people. The fruit can also be used in the making of jams and honey, although here again, it is never likely to be in great demand.

2. *Market Huckleberry* (*Gaylussacia baccata*)

Closely allied to the *vacciniums* there are many species of *gaylussacia*, which are deciduous members of the *ericaceae* family. Natives of South America they should be grown in unexposed positions so that they escape injury in case of prolonged severe winter weather. The majority of species have black fruits. *Gaylussacia baccata* has the common name of partridge berry and although the edible berries are quite tasty, it is unlikely these shrubby plants will ever be grown on a large scale. Even so, the fruit is frequently seen on the markets.

Gaylussacia frondosa is the dangleberry having blue berries, others include *Gaylussacia dumosa, Gaylussacia resinosa* and *Gaylussacia ursina* none of which are particularly striking although once established they usually berry freely.

Propagation is by cuttings in summer of semi-ripe shoots placed in the shady frame where the soil is of a sandy-peaty mixture or layers can be made in autumn, while division is satisfactory in September or March. Alternatively, seed can be sown in moist sandy peat in a temperature of $12°-14°C.$ ($55°-60°F.$) in spring.

JAPANESE WINEBERRY (*Rubus phoeniciolasius*)

Introduced to Britain from Japan and Korea in 1876, this fruit has never attained the popularity it deserves. It is of value for its fruits which are rarely if ever attacked by birds, and for its highly decorative appearance. It can be grown as a bush by keeping the stems topped when about 1.5 m (5 ft.) high and cutting back the laterals to about 60 cm (2 ft.). This treatment leads to the development of really large specimens which remain satisfactory so long as the canes that have fruited are cut out each autumn in the same way as for raspberries.

Alternatively, the plants can be allowed to make long growths like those of loganberries. In this case too, annual pruning is essential to prevent unwanted and unproductive 'wood'.

The stems are covered with soft red hairs while the flowers are quite ornamental. The fruits, which turn an orange colour at first, gradually change to blood-red when they are ripe. Fairly small not much more than half the size of a large raspberry, the slightly acid flavour is quite good especially if eaten with cream.

Propagation is easy from tip layering in autumn.

KINGS ACRE BERRY
A hybrid between the blackberry and raspberry, this is early maturing, the sturdy canes bearing heavy crops of long-shaped black berries of splendid flavour.

LOGANBERRY
It was nearly one hundred years ago when in the garden of Judge Logan of California, there occurred a natural cross between a variety of raspberry and a form of American blackberry. Although some authorities doubt this, no other possibility has ever been put forward. This hybrid, which was named the loganberry, was introduced into Great Britain well over seventy-five years ago. It has been grown under varying conditions and has proved to be absolutely hardy and an abundant bearer. The large, dark red berries ripen in the summer and the crop is produced over a period of many weeks. The juicy fruit is of good flavour, being specially valuable for stewing and jam-making.

It is essential to grow a good stock. Perhaps the reason that the loganberry is not always valued as much as it ought to be, is due to poor stocks being grown. These sometimes arise as variant seedlings, which are similar in appearance to the original and one has even seen them growing in commercial plantations. Generally, they possess indifferent cropping qualities and have poor disease resistance, which can give the plant a bad reputation.

When grown well, the true loganberry will yield heavily. Although some people like the fruit when it is ripe for dessert, it is not to everybody's taste, since it lacks the sweetness of both the blackberry and raspberry. It is, however, suitable for cooking purposes, jam-making and bottling, as well as fruit juice manufacture. Loganberries ripen from July onwards.

Planting can be carried out from November until March, the normal spacing being 2.4 m (6–8 ft.) apart. The canes should be cut back after planting, to encourage strong basal growths to develop. These should be tied into place and not left to flop about, for it is on the new canes that fruit is borne.

Where a good vigorous stock is available, it can be propagated by tip layers. For this the young canes should be bent over during July and August, the tips being well-firmed into the soil. They can remain in position until the following spring, when they should be moved to nursery beds. After a year, they will be good, strong specimens, suitable for planting out or for sale the following season. A mulch of good strawy manure or compost each spring will encourage heavier crops.

Once the tips have been severed and planted up, the parent stock plants should be cut back to within 10 cm (4 in.) of the ground. A new set of canes will then develop and furnish further suitable material for propagation.

The thornless loganberry was introduced to Britain well over thirty years ago. The fruit is large and good-flavoured, excellent for stewing and jam-making. Growth is strong and of attractive appearance, and the culture is the same as for the ordinary loganberry. This is the best variety to grow where training is difficult.

MEDLAR *(Mespilus germanica)*
A native of Southern Europe and belonging to the rose family, the medlar is now known in all parts of the world and is to be found both in a wild and cultivated state. At one time this tree was to be found in the gardens and grounds of any estate of consequence and the fruit was considered indispensable when used in sauces and served with game.

The trees vary in size and appearance which is probably influenced by both soil and climatic conditions. Generally, the trunk is on the short side and is rough. The branches are crooked and irregular in shape, being rather spreading, while the wild specimens are well furnished with thorns. The bark of nearly all varieties is of an ash-grey colour.

In the early summer the tree is made quite showy by reason of the large white blossoms. The medlar is a grafted tree, several stocks being used for this purpose. *Quince* is very suitable for fairly moist soils, whereas *Whitethorn* is a reliable stock where the trees are to be grown on dry land.

Seed is another means of propagation, but in this case, there is a waiting period of at least two years and chiefly because of this, it is better for the grower to concentrate on grafted or budded trees.

Where large standard medlars are required, seedling pear stocks may be used, grafting them at the height required so as to produce a good, straight stem.

The fruits of medlars which are more or less round have a slight depression at the top and are crowned by the sepals of the calyx, giving them a distinctive appearance. They are generally reddish-brown in colour and contain five hard, rather rugged kernels. When the fruit ripens towards the end of the autumn, it has an astringent taste. It is therefore usual and advisable to allow them to remain on the trees, gathering them during November, after they have been exposed to some frosts but not to really severe weather.

They are ready for picking when their stalks part readily from the shoots. Gathered then and kept in a dry frost-proof place, they should be laid on straw or a rack, remaining there for a few weeks when they become pleasant to eat, having a mellow somewhat vinous flavour.

The fruit yielded by really old trees becomes small and flavourless, although medlars are sometimes grown for their odd, yet handsome appearance and the showiness of their blooms, the fruit being disregarded.

Though hard when gathered, the fruit soon becomes soft. The best way to store the fruits is to place them eye downwards. From two to four weeks will be required for them to change from green to yellow, this process being known as bletting. They are then ready for use, and will remain so for several weeks. Though not to everyone's taste, in addition to being eaten raw, medlars may be made into jam, jelly or sauce. To lessen any possibility of the fruit rotting in store, it should be gathered during dry, sunny weather. Some growers have found that the dipping of the end of the stalks in a solution of ordinary table salt, will reduce or even prevent rotting.

As with other fruit trees, well-shaped specimens are produced by early training and pruning, in order to form an open, evenly branched head. Once this has been obtained, subsequent treatment consists of removing dead wood and rubbing out badly placed shoots.

Medlars are not subject to any particular pests or diseases. Occasion-

ally leaf-eating weevils are troublesome in the spring, but they can be controlled by a thorough dusting or spraying of derris or pyrethrum.
Varieties

Nottingham is of upright habit. The fruit is on the small side, but is freely produced and when ripe has a rich sub-acid flavour.

Royal is also of upright growth, a heavy cropper of medium size and good flavour. It has received a first-class certificate from the Royal Horticultural Society.

The *Dutch,* also known as *Monster,* forms a decorative tree with large leaves and a semi-weeping habit. It has brownish fruits which remain in good condition longer than other sorts, often keeping until the New Year.

MELON *(Cucumis melo)*
Although annuals, no reference to soft fruits would be complete without melons, which produce variously shaped and coloured fruits. They have been in cultivation for centuries and are easy to manage when grown in favourable positions and where they have full light although there must be shade from direct sun.

Seed should be sown in heated frames in April or on hotbeds of about 22°C. (75°F.) using pots or boxes. A mixture of loam and peat is suitable, a little wood ash and old mortar rubble being useful additions.

Place the seed edgeways, 12 mm (½ in.) deep, and keep the frames closed until germination occurs. Provide ventilation and water as necessary and when the seedlings have two leaves, move them to the frame or Dutch light, where a hotbed has been prepared. Handle them with care and give some shade until they are established.

Collar rot and *root rot* are sometimes a trouble. It is an advantage to plant on slightly raised soil to prevent moisture collecting around the base of the stem at soil level and regular ventilation is an important factor in the culture of melons.

Frequent syringings of water will help in providing a moist atmosphere. When the plants have formed three leaves, pinch out the leading shoot preferably when it is sunny, to encourage quick healing. Once laterals have formed four leaves, they too, are stopped about the third leaf. It is on the sub-laterals that the fruit is borne.

Plants produce male and female flowers, the latter being recognized by a small swelling at the base of the petals. The male pollen-bearing flowers, are smaller.

Pollen has to be transferred to the female flower. This is often done by bees but early in the season and with frame plants, it is advisable to do it by hand. It is done by picking the male flower and lightly rubbing the pollen on to the stigma in the centre of the female flower.

The best time for this job is between 12 noon and 2 p.m. preferably when it is sunny. Pollinate all the female flowers the same day when they are fully open and dry. After a few days, the swelling at the back of each female flower will begin to enlarge. When the fruitlets are the size of a walnut, select the best and cut off the remainder at one leaf above the fruit. Keep the vines growing so that each has plenty of room and does not become crowded.

Plants can also be placed in the cold frame or under cloches from the middle to the end of April. Prepare a good hole for each plant, filling it with well-rotted manure. Plant the melon on a little ridge to avoid the roots becoming waterlogged.

Cutting begins in August when signs of ripening are cracks on the fruit near the stalk, deep colour and a real melon aroma. To avoid reducing flavour, do not water the plants when the fruits start to ripen.

The group known as Canteloupe melons are the easiest to manage. These include *Dutch Net* and *Tiger,* the latter being especially reliable and self-fertile. For growing with little or no heat, there is *No Name* (an odd title!) also the F.1. hybrid, *Burpee Hybrid,* which has rounded golden-netted fruit and thick juicy orange flesh. *Sweetheart* is another splendid F.1. hybrid with salmon-pink flesh. It does well in frames or under cloches. *Charantais* is a small, delicious variety with scented flesh. Of the varieties of melons needing heated or warm greenhouse treatment, *King George, Hero of Lockinge, Superlative* and the green-fleshed *Emerald Green* are most dependable.

Water Melons can be grown where a little heat is available, while they are hardy enough for frame and cloche cultivation. With heat, they can be grown in the same way as the Cantaloupes. Without warmth, sow the seed in April using pots of peaty compost standing them in the cold frame. When the seedlings are ready for their fruiting positions select

[61]

sandy soil, well-mulched with good compost. Set the plants on little mounds about 75 cm (2½ ft.) apart, remembering that the plants will not be bushy specimens but will be kept to one main stem growing 1.5 m (5 ft.) or more. Make sure water does not settle round the plants or stem rot will develop.

Shallow furrows can be made both sides of the plants. These can be flooded as necessary during the summer or clay pots can be sunk in the soil near the plants and these can be frequently filled with water. After the fruits have set, carefully place them on pieces of asbestos or something similar to prevent slug or other pest damage.

Water melons are ready for cutting when the tendrils near the ripening fruits become dry and shrivelled. *Florida Favourite* is good, the oval fruits are of six pounds or more, having green skin and pink flesh.

MULBERRY *(Morus nigra)*

Although not usually classed among the soft fruits, the mulberry comes into this group since the fruit is soft as opposed to apples, pears, etc.

As both ornamental and fruiting trees, black mulberries possess considerable merit, for although they are usually thought of on account of their fruiting ability, they are of attractive appearance whether in fruit or not. They are almost always grown as standards, bushes not being satisfactory because of the spreading habit of the branches.

The mulberry likes a good sandy loam, well supplied with moisture, but certainly not a waterlogged position. An open, sunny situation is preferred, in fact if given the same conditions as plums, they will usually do well. It is important to remember, that although the tree may be comparatively small at planting time, and it grows slowly at first, it will develop into quite a big specimen, after a few years.

Good deep soil preparation is advisable, working in well-rotted manure and compost, while bone meal applied at the rate of 113 g (4 oz.) per square metre will do good. Lime does not appear to be essential, although mulberries succeed where it is present. Planting time is from the middle of October until the end of March, the earlier the better.

Where more than one tree is being planted, up to 9 m (30 ft.) should be allowed between them, to allow for eventual development. It is necessary to spread out the roots fully, and not to cramp or damage them by putting them in holes which are too small. They should be covered with about 13 cm (5 in.) of soil above the roots, and staking should for preference, be done before the tree is put in.

Early transplanting is important, and this is why young trees of three or four years will move better than older specimens. Pruning in the initial stages consists of shortening all leading growths by about a third, and cutting back the laterals to within a couple of buds from the base. Because mulberries are somewhat slow in coming into bearing, it is advisable to start with trees which are about five years old.

Once the main framework is formed, very little further pruning is needed. This makes early training so important, and any later cutting should be done immediately after leaf-fall. Since isolated mulberries are sometimes seen fruiting heavily, it is obvious that this subject is self-fertile, in fact, really established trees regularly bear heavy crops of sweet, curious-looking fruit.

The shape of the leaves varies from tree to tree, while quite often, leaves on the upper branches are different from those on the lower ones. Mulberries are among the latest trees to produce foliage in the spring, but they are most showy in the late summer, when most other trees are beginning to lose their attractiveness for the season. The fruit ripens over a period of some weeks. This spread of production, is apt to obscure the considerable quantities that an individual tree will bear. The fruit is ready for gathering when it assumes a dark crimson colour, which it does throughout August and September. If the berries cannot be used as soon as they are ready, they can be bottled.

Mulberries may be propagated in various ways, the simplest method being by layering. In this case, healthy young branches are selected and pegged into the ground in the autumn. They should remain there until the following autumn, when they are severed, having by that time made a good root system.

Cuttings can be made from young shoots, these should be taken in October and be about 30–45 cm (12–18 in.) long. They should be prepared in the usual way, and buried firmly 13–15 cm (5–6 in.) deep in sandy soil in a sheltered place. Cuttings are often difficult to root and hormone powder or solution is sometimes used. Grafting can be done in

March. This consists of selecting suitable shoots from trees of good form, and working them on strong seedling mulberries.

Seed is another way of obtaining stock, and it should be sown in good compost in March. Germination is often irregular and this means that some years elapse before fruiting trees are available.

The fruiting or black mulberry, *Morus nigra* is, of course, quite distinct from *Morus alba,* the white mulberry, which is grown for its leaves which are used for silkworms.

NECTARBERRY

A seedling from the youngberry, it matures earlier than that hybrid and is also a little earlier ripening than the boysenberry. It goes on fruiting intermittently over a long period, the berries being softer to the taste than most others.

RASPBERRY *(Rubus ideaus)*

The wild raspberry, *Rubus idaeus* is to be found in many places, not only in Britain but in other European and Asian countries as well. From these have come many splendid cultivated and named varieties.

They produce many fibrous roots and prefer a rich medium-heavy soil, but this must be well-drained and contain plenty of humus. Very light ground, unless generously manured before planting and mulched annually, will produce crops poor in weight and quality. On these soils too, there is often a lack of potash which shows itself in the scorched edges of the leaves. This shortage can be remedied by a dressing of a good organic fertilizer, while bonfire ash placed along the rows and lightly pricked-in is helpful. Sulphate of potash is sometimes sprinkled along the sides of the rows but not on the crowns of the canes.

Sites are important and if possible, the rows should run north to south. An open, sunny but not exposed position is best. Frost pockets and other low-lying ground should be avoided, otherwise the flowers may be damaged and some of the prospective crop lost. As with other soft fruits, the ground should be cleared of weeds before planting is done. If not, it will be very difficult to get rid of tenacious weeds such as bindweed, couch grass and convolvulus.

Planting can be done from October onwards. Autumn planting is best since by the early spring the basal shoots are developing and may easily be broken off. Even so, many gardeners do plant successfully up until April. According to space available and the strength of the variety, the rows can be 1.5–2.1 m (5–7 ft.) apart. Allow 38–60 cm (15–24 in.) between the canes, again according to variety, for some do produce a spreading root system and form many new canes. Some gardeners like to keep each 'stool' separate, instead of letting them grow into each other. Plant firmly but not deeply. The best guide is the soil mark on the canes being planted, the new soil being brought just above this mark to allow for natural sinkage.

Newly planted canes should be cut down to 23 cm (9 in.). This operation can be delayed until the very early spring. No fruit should be taken the first year after planting. Suckers will be produced during the summer and it is these that will fruit the following season.

To keep the growths tidy and make it easy for gathering the fruit, it is necessary to provide some means of support. The simplest method is to erect posts at each end of the rows with wires running between them. Two strands of wire will be needed, the lowest 90 cm (3 ft.) from ground level with the top one about 1.5 m (5 ft.) from the soil. Where weaker growing varieties are planted, the two strands can be lower. Since a number of canes will develop from each stool, they should be trained so that they are spaced about 15 cm (6 in.) apart on the wires. Soft fillis or raffia ties are very effective.

A mulch of manure or compost in May or early June will ensure the roots do not dry out just when the fruit is developing. Once fruiting is finished cut out all canes which have carried fruit. Four canes should be regarded as ample for each stool, any others should be removed. Propagation is by suckers which arise from the extensive root system. Because of virus diseases it is advisable to stick to Ministry certified varieties when buying stock, although this does not mean that other healthy stocks do not exist.

Raspberries are usually plugged when picked, except if the fruit is being exhibited, or if it is being sent or taken on a journey. If the berries are picked before they are quite ripe, they will keep for a day or so without deteriorating. Keep the rows well-picked, as over-ripe fruit on

E

the canes is soon affected with grey mould fungus which spreads quite quickly.

As soon as the crop of good berries has been gathered malformed and maggoty specimens should not be left on the canes but should be picked and destroyed. Otherwise, the grubs drop to the ground and hibernate until the next season when they begin their attack again.

Pruning should then begin. It consists of cutting down to ground level all the old canes from which fruit has been gathered. Their early removal allows light and air to reach and ripen the young canes. It is best to burn all prunings since these old canes being more or less hollow, offer suitable hiding places for pests to hibernate.

Once the old canes have been cut out, the new ones should be thinned to prevent over-crowding. First take out weak and unhealthy looking growths and as necessary, thin out the remainder. Especially if the raspberries are being grown on wires or trellis supports, the aim should be to allow about 13 cm (5 in.) between the canes. Grown without supports, seven canes each stool is quite sufficient and subsequently, all suckers arising out of row-alignment should be pulled out.

Raspberry stools do not go on indefinitely like apples or pears and after five or six years they begin to deteriorate, losing vigour and cropping ability. To prevent a year's loss of crop a row of new young canes should be planted the year before the old stools are to be destroyed. These new canes will then come into fruiting the year the stools are taken up. As a rule, it is best to obtain an entirely new stock rather than selecting young canes from the old bed to start the new plantation.

There are a few pests that attack raspberries, the worst being the maggots of the *Raspberry Beetle*. These burrow into the plug of the fruit as well as feeding on the drupelets. It is therefore important to deal with them before they create damage. This can be done by using the non-poisonous liquid derris, the first application being applied about the second week in June with a second one towards the end of the month.

Aphides or greenflies are also troublesome at times, and liquid derris can be used for these too. The *Raspberry Moth* is capable of causing considerable losses. The result of the attacks is seen from April onwards when many of the young shoots particularly those at the top of the cane, will be found to be withering and dying.

On examination, it will be seen that the inside of the shoots have been eaten away and quite often a small red caterpillar can be found inside the tunnel in the shoot. Later there will be the brown chrysalis. If a lot of shoots are attacked, it will cause considerable loss since no flowers will be produced.

The Raspberry Moth is a small insect having dark purplish-brown wings which often shine and have on them a number of conspicuous yellow spots. These moths appear at the end of May and June and lay their eggs in the raspberry flowers.

After a week or so, young whitish caterpillars hatch out from the eggs and burrow into the plug of the fruit on which they feed. Very often it is difficult to tell whether or not they are in the fruit.

One of the problems in regard to the Raspberry Moth is, that the caterpillars leave the fruits when they begin to ripen and find places where they make cocoons in which to spend the winter. These are often placed in crevices on the old canes or on the stakes and sometimes too, in the soil around the stools.

In early April the caterpillars emerge from their cocoons and crawl up the canes to the shoots in which they burrow to start the process all over again. It is important at all times, to keep the canes free from rubbish and all supports should also be cleaned, also places where the pests can hibernate. The spraying of the canes and stakes with tar oil winter wash seems to be quite effective and this can be done while the canes are dormant and certainly up to the end of February. It pays to keep a watch on raspberry beds so that all withered shoots which may contain grubs or chrysalides can be destroyed early in the spring as soon as they are seen.

If straw is used as a mulch, this too, should be sprayed. Although they rarely occur where straw mulching is used, sometimes raspberry canes are attacked by *cane blight* and *blue striped wilt*. For these a colloidal copper wash should be sprayed on in the early spring as soon as the buds begin to swell.

Varieties

Lloyd George is still the most popular and widely grown variety, being quite remarkable for its perpetual fruiting habit, going on from early summer to late autumn. The large fruit is of wonderful flavour and firm

[67]

texture, and it is one of the best for 'travelling' and therefore valued by market growers. Unfortunately, it has become susceptible to virus diseases during the last few years, resulting in stunted growth, yellowing foliage and loss of crop. But where a healthy stock is grown, Lloyd George can still take the leading place for good quality. New stock saved from individual clones that are virus resistant are now readily available and can be planted with confidence. It is certain that the popularity of this variety will remain as great as ever.

Newburgh is a good mid-season sort of execellent dessert quality, but it has never become very popular. Perhaps this is because the canes are frequently victims of blight with its unhappy results.

Norfolk Giant introduced about thirty years ago, is another fine sort. The medium-sized, bright red, firm, juicy fruit is later-ripening than many of the sorts mentioned, while it is valuable for preserving. When introduced this variety soon became popular, but on account of its sensitivity to virus infection, which readily shows itself by the mottled and irregularly developed foliage, it has lost some favour, although it is easy to see any plants affected by the discolouration of the leaves and dwarf growth of the canes.

Preussen is another old variety which is not widely grown although it is of good flavour.

Pyne's Imperial is reckoned by some growers to be an improved Royal. A strong grower, it has the same good flavour and if anything is a heavier cropper than Pyne's Royal.

Pyne's Royal, is an old variety which has been grown for sixty years and has received an Award of Merit from the Royal Horticultural Society and is particularly large-fruited. The flavour is good, the berries firm and juicy, and it is altogether an excellent variety for both dessert and preserving purposes.

Red Cross is another strong growing sort, doing well where soil conditions are not good. It is early fruiting, rich and juicy and particularly valuable for jam-making.

St. Walfried is fairly well-known. A good cropper of medium-quality fruits, it is sometimes susceptible to virus disease.

A group of varieties raised at the East Malling Research Station are proving to be remarkable croppers, especially when grown on land rich in humus. The first of these and incidently one of the earliest of all is *Malling Promise* with large firm berries of good colour and flavour, being ready for picking in mid-June. In exposed places only, the freely produced canes may suffer from frost damage. In such circumstances it is best to grow *Malling Exploit* which is disease resistant and a very heavy cropper of good flavour. It is ten to fourteen days later than Promise.

Malling Jewel is the next to mature and already has a good reputation. Of good colour and flavour it travels well and seems to thrive under all conditions. *Malling Notable* follows and is remarkable for its very large berries and good appearance making it specially suitable for exhibition. If anything this variety is not quite so strong growing as the two Malling sorts just mentioned. It seems to like some protection from strong winds. Ready for gathering in mid-July, *Malling Enterprise* is another heavy cropper although it does not seem to produce new canes as freely as the others. It is ideal for preserving and well worth growing. The latest of the Malling sorts is *Landmark* which yields a good crop well into August. Since it is late-flowering its value for growing in districts subjected to late frosts will be easily appreciated although the quality of the fruit is not so good as the earlier sorts.

Malling Admiral is a valuable late season variety, reckoned to be superior to Norfolk Giant. The fruits are large and firm, of excellent flavour, the colour being dark red. They are easily plugged. The tall canes grow strong and numerous and this is why they are best grown in fairly sheltered sites. *Malling Orion* is a heavy yielding mid-season variety, resistant to many strains of aphides which means that they usually escape aphis-borne diseases. The firm fruits are of medium size and of good flavour. They are first-class for canning and freezing, but less satisfactory for jamming. The canes are tall and strong and sometimes branch in the upper half.

Glen Clova is a fairly new early-ripening variety cropping over a long period. Of excellent flavour it is valued for dessert, jam, bottling and freezing.

Among the autumn-fruiting sorts Lloyd George must be included for it frequently goes on bearing until October or later. Others are *Hailsham* a very excellent variety with large dark red fruit of high quality, while *November Abundance* is of medium size, the dark red fruits being sweet and juicy. *September* is an unusual firm, red variety cropping in September.

Of the yellow raspberries *Antwerp,* although introduced well over a century ago is still very good and in fair demand. It is a fine grower, freely producing large, roundish berries of really nice flavour.

There are also a few autumn-fruiting yellow sorts. *Exeter Yellow* produces a good crop of very sweet, rich-coloured fruit and *Lord Lambourne* is a splendid sort, rather like Lloyd George excepting colour. *Fallgold* is a new golden-yellow autumn-fruiting raspberry bearing a heavy crop of sweet large berries over a long period.

Zeva is known as the perpetual-fruiting raspberry of Swiss origin. It fruits on young canes from July until November. The berries being very large and of superb flavour.

Among really old varieties rarely available today are the following.

Bath's Perfection This is said to be synonymous with several varieties including *Laxton's Abundance* and *Marlborough.* The large round fruit is a bright red colour and of excellent flavour. The strong growing canes which fruit heavily, have a reddish-purple colour.

Baumforth's Seedling is a splendid commercial variety which has long been grown on a large scale in Scotland. The large firm berries are of sweet flavour and the canes strong growing and producing good crops.

Brown's Seedling This was raised in Ireland and in many respects is like Lloyd George, the medium-sized sweet fruit being good for both dessert and jam-making.

Chartham This is a comparatively new sort raised at Chartham in Kent. The large fruit of good flavour, is normally available from June to well into August.

Corfe Mullen Wonder As the name suggest, this originated in Dorset and is said to be a strain of Lloyd George. The large well-flavoured fruit is produced over a very long period and it is a variety which is often grown for its autumn crop.

RHUBARB *(Rheum rhaponticum)*

A native of China its history can be traced back to several thousand years BC. Various species have taken part in the production of rhubarb as we know it to-day and through the course of time the plant has been gradually improved. Although its food value is not great, rhubarb is appreciated early in the year before fresh fruit becomes available. The plant has medicinal value and was originally used solely for this purpose. The leaves are not edible since they contain oxalic acid.

An easy plant to grow, it will remain productive for many years. It is a pity that rhubarb is often grown in positions which are badly drained or where the soil is poor. Deeply move the soil since the plants make thick branching roots. If stable and farmyard manure and compost are worked-in they will provided feeding material over a long period. Bone meal and wood ashes are also useful. For earliest outdoor rhubarb, a fairly sheltered position is required.

Plant from autumn to spring when the soil is workable. Allow 90 cm (3 ft.) between the crowns for they increase in size and need ample room. Spread the roots fully, planting firmly, covering the crowns with 5 cm (2 in.) of soil. Do not pull any stalks the first season and in subsequent years always leave some stalks on each plant.

It is best not to pull much after mid-summer excepting in the case of stalks needed for jam- or wine-making. Rhubarb should not be cut but gripped at the base of the stem and pulled with a jerking movement. Flower heads should always be removed. To keep the plants productive, give a dressing of manure annually. Inverted pots or boxes placed over some of the plants will provide outdoor pullings.

Rhubarb is sometimes affected by *crown rot* in which the stem bases become swollen and distorted and spindly useless shoots develop. All infected plants should be burnt with the soil immediately surrounding them.

Varieties include, *Prince Albert, Linnaeus* and *Victoria*. If one or more of these are grown it will provide a natural succession of sticks for pulling from April onwards. It is possible to raise rhubarb from seed and *Glaskin's Perpetual* is one of the best for this purpose and matures quickly.

Forcing rhubarb While it is usual to force three year-old plants, rather younger specimens can be used, provided they are strong and healthy. Plants to be grown in this way should not be pulled during the summer, so that their strength will be directed entirely to building up sturdy crowns for producing a good crop when forced.

The simplest way to force rhubarb is under the heated greenhouse staging. Sacks or hessian draped in front of the staging will provide the necessary darkness. Should hot water pipes be under the staging, it is best to stand boards or other screens in front so that dry heat does not directly reach the rhubarb.

Timing is important. If the aim is to produce sticks for Christmas, forcing should commence five weeks previously. To maintain a succession, batches of crowns must be bought in at fourteen-day intervals. Make sure that the soil is nicely moist before planting.

Pack the crowns closely together, filling the spaces between them with sandy loam, fine peat or leaf mould so there are no air pockets. Once planted, the crowns should be given a good soaking with water. To begin with a temperature of 8°C. (45°F.) is adequate but a week later it should be raised to 10°C. (50°F.) and after a further eight to ten days to 15°–18°C. (60°–65°F.)

For forcing, *Champagne* and *Dawes Champion* are good varieties, whilst *The Sutton* is also reliable.

STRAWBERRY *(Fragaria chiloensis)*

There are a number of wild European species of strawberries. At least some of them have been known and recorded for more than 500 years. The exact origin of the modern strawberry is somewhat confused but among species that have played a part in giving size, flavour and other good qualities are *Fragaria chiloensis, Fragaria elatior* and *Fragaria virginiana.*

As far as the so-called alpine strawberries are concerned *Fragaria viridis* and *Fragaria vesca* are among the ancestors of the present day varieties. One of the unusual characteristics of the strawberry is that its seeds are produced on the outside of the fruit instead of the inside as in the case of nearly all other edible plants.

The strawberry is one of the most important of the soft fruits and many thousands of acres of plants are cultivated commercially. In addition they are grown in private gardens in all parts of the British Isles and of course, in other countries too. They are not everybody's fruit. To some they give a rash, to others twinges of rheumatism, though the latter is very, very less likely if the berries are ripe before being eaten.

For preference the plants should be grown in a rich, medium loam, plentifully supplied with humus matter. Drainage must be good and the roots should not dry out during spring droughts for that is just the time when moisture is required to encourage the berries to set and swell. This is why the organic content of the soil should be maintained. The making of a really good bed will be well rewarded by the size of the crop and the quality of the berries. While light sandy soils will produce reasonable crops, on shallow chalky ground, the plants become weak, the leaves pale and the crop poor.

When making a new bed plenty of organic material such as decayed manure, compost, leaf mould, peat and shoddy should be worked in. While it is true that chemical fertilizers can be used to provide the minerals required by the plants, they cannot be recommended without reserve. Their continued use leads to a thin, lifeless, powdery soil lacking bulk and unable to hold moisture.

Among the major mineral elements and compounds needed by strawberries if they are to develop properly, are phosphates, potassium, nitrates, magnesium and iron, with many of the trace elements. In a really good soil, the roots can gather and use just what they need. Where some of these properties are missing, the plants and often the fruit are bound to be of lower quality.

Since strawberries are so low growing, they are subject to frost damage. Therefore the site is important. An exposed, windswept position should be avoided although one is bound to say that in open, hedgeless fields in East Anglia and elsewhere there is usually remarkably little damage. The danger period is from the end of April to mid-June and probably the reason there is often less damage from frosts than one would expect, is because by that time, the rows have usually been strawed in readiness for the developing fruit.

Frost damage is indicated by a black eye or centre to the flower caused by the killing of the stigma and ovules. There can be no recovery from this damage. Wherever possible avoid making the strawberry bed in a low situation. Such positions far from being warmer, act as frost pockets. Cutting winds will sometimes cause the discoloration of the foliage. In the case of small beds, it will not be unduly troublesome to sprinkle

[73]

straw or place light mats over the plants should there be signs of frost when the blossoms are opening.

The planting site must be prepared well in advance for a firm, well settled soil is essential if the plants are to make a good start and do well. It should be weed-free too, for once the strawberries are in the ground, it will not be possible to do any deep cultivation. The earlier that planting can be done the better, August and the first few days of September is a really good period although satisfactory results can be secured by planting as late as November. With late plantings there is the possibility of some winter losses.

One of the drawbacks of the modern certification schemes is that the health certificates cannot be issued until fairly late in the year. This is because any possible virus symptoms do not show until then. The nurseryman is therefore bound to be late in lifting and despatching the plants where a new stock is being bought.

It is of course quite safe to plant in the spring, in fact some specialists do plant in March and April if the job cannot be done by the first week in October. At planting time, the soil should be in a nice workable condition, breaking down well. A trowel should be used when putting in the plants. This will make it possible to arrange for a good hole to be scooped out to allow the roots to spread out fully. As to spacing 38–45 cm (15–18 in.) apart with 60–75 cm (2–2½ ft.) between rows is about right. If the year following planting you intend to root runners between the rows, the spacing can be 30–38 cm (12–15 in.) between plants with the rows up to 90 cm (3 ft.) apart. By planting in August and September a good crop should be secured the following spring. In addition, there will be some good strong young runners.

Plants used for making new beds are of course maidens, that is, very young plants. Often they are only a few weeks old. They can come directly from the open ground or may be pot plants. If plants show signs of flagging following planting they should be watered daily until established. In spring droughts a few soakings at the time the berries are swelling will be helpful. After the bed has been made, all cultivation should be shallow, since the plants are surface rooting. When the ground is cleaned between the rows, draw the soil toward the crowns but do not cover them. If a mulch of peat is applied as the soil begins to warm up in the spring, it will both smother weeds and provide valuable extra organic matter for the surface soil. If the remains of the straw applied for the protection of the fruit is not burned off, a practice frequently carried out by commercial growers, it can be lightly forked in during the autumn, that is unless there has been trouble with pests and diseases. In that case, the straw and old foliage can be burned off.

As to the feeding of established strawberry beds, the plants react marvellously to organic fertilizers. Well-rotted manure, while so invaluable for digging-in when preparing the bed, is not so suitable once the plants are growing, although some growers do spread manure or compost over the entire bed. There are several types of suitable surface fertilizers. Some gardeners use 14 g (½ oz.) of sulphate of potash and sulphate of ammonia, and 28 g (1 oz.) of superphosphate of lime, to each square metre of bed. It is far better, in my opinion, to use bone flour, fish meal or hoof and horn manure, at the rate of 85–113 g (3–4 ozs.) to the square metre. These are more expensive, but give better results. It is satisfactory to use in the spring, or after fruiting, or half the quantities recommended could be used at both times. The advantage of applying fertilizer after picking the fruit is that it helps to build up the crowns for the next year's crop.

taken the first year. This is rather a hard thing to expect the gardener to do, for most of us like to have at least a sample crop the first year. De-blossoming certainly allows the plants to become thoroughly established and heavier crops will be secured the following season. The blossom trusses should not be pulled out, but cut off with scissors or a sharp knife.

Strawberries are easy to propagate. Although plants can be raised from seed, generally speaking it is not worth the trouble, unless one intends to experiment. Seed does not produce plants true to type. The modern varieties are complex hybrids, not all characters being fixed. It might be possible to raise a variety from seed having most of the sought-after qualities and few faults. For this, one would need to use two first class parents having the qualities desired. The drawback is that the result of crossing two first class varieties might very well be that at least some of the good points might be lost and undesirable traits from generations back might be brought to light.

Forcing Strawberries

Strawberry plants from which runners are to be used for forcing must be rooted, preferably in pots, at the earliest date possible. They should be encouraged to grow sturdily by keeping them well supplied with moisture in summer. Runner beds can be planted in partial shade, for instance between two rows of trees. Plants for producing runners should be carefully selected before planting and only used once for the production of runners.

Throughout the whole season of runner-production for forcing, the flowers and secondary runners are constantly removed from the plants. As soon as the runners show some root formation, they are carefully lifted without being separated from the old plant and after shortening the roots they are potted in medium 60's (8 cm) which are plunged in the runner bed. The potting compost must be rich and have a high moisture-retaining capacity. A mixture of turfy loam, well-rotted manure, some sharp sand and a good general fertilizer would be most suitable.

The runners are not separated from the old plants until they are really well established in the pots. The root pruning given before potting, the rich compost and the moist, shady atmosphere will ensure that the runners can be taken off the old plants at least one month earlier than if the plants are not touched.

Plants for forcing should be potted separately in August or as soon after as possible. When ready they should be placed directly into size 32 (16 cm) clay pots, each one having a crock with a piece of turf above, placed at the base to assist drainage. A potting compost of good loam, decayed manure, silver sand and a sprinkling of bone meal is very suitable or the John Innes No. 3 can be used. This should be well-firmed at planting time with the crown of the plant left just clear of the soil which should not fill the pot completely. Leave about 12 cm (1 in.) of the inside showing which will assist proper watering.

For the first two days after potting keep the pots on level ground (preferably overlaid with grit or ashes) in a semi-shaded position. They can then be exposed to full light so that the leaf area can begin to manufacture food and to build up general development. Do not allow pots to dry out and do not over-water. In October, stack the pots on their sides in a cold frame removing the lights in periods of dry weather.

Alternatively place them at the base of a sheltered wall protecting the pots from cracking during severe frosty weather.

In January transfer to the glasshouse bench. The glasshouse temperature should be raised gradually, and the night temperature held at up to, but never over, 10°C. (50°F.). The day temperature can be around 15°C. (60°F.).

Flowering should commence around mid-March and hand-pollinating with soft cotton wool or a rabbit's or hare's tail is worthwhile. If conditions of sunlight are favourable extra ventilation during the blossoming period, should be given. Aim at giving as much as possible so long as the temperature is held steady.

After fruit setting commences, aim at the higher temperature of 20°C. (70°F.) during the day, and 15°C. (60°F.) at night. Some assistance to the plant can be made at this time by applying diluted blood meal, soot water, or any recommended organic liquid manure. If the plants appear to be growing well, and are of good colour, feeding is unnecessary for it could lead to over-stimulation. Keep a watch for greenfly, red spider, and any similar pests. Under different trade names the appropriate control materials are available, from most horticultural suppliers and garden centres. Spraying with a derris or pyrethrum base is most suitable and safest.

Birds of course should be kept out of the greenhouse and we have known of mice acquiring a special interest in glasshouse strawberries.

The very early strawberry crops which often have to be produced in damp, dull weather are the most difficult to bring on. Hormones, artificial illumination and sugar sprays can be called upon to assist. Hormone sprays are mainly used on crops in glasshouses or on framed crops which have been damaged by frost. Normally, the cost of application on a frame crop of strawberries does not justify its use. The hormones are applied to the flowers in a finely divided spray, ensuring that as little as possible lands on the foliage. Several applications at five day intervals may be necessary if the flowering period extends over any length of time.

Artificial irradiation is effective on early strawberries, but the cost of its use is often prohibitive except perhaps for the very early crops. If it is used, then white fluorescent strip-lighting of 40 watts gives good results. The tubes are fitted 60 cm (2 ft.) above the plants, one tube per square metre of bench and the plants are irradiated for five hours every night.

A better and certainly a much cheaper method, is the use of sugar sprays. The spray consists of a 10% solution of ordinary sugar to which 0.025% of sulphanylamide is added as a deterrent against fungal growth. The spray is given at weekly intervals, starting as soon as the plants have resumed growth after housing. The plants should be thoroughly moistened with the spray. Particularly on very early crops this treatment has been most satisfactory and has given 20% and 25% increases in the yield.

Propagation

The usual way of propagating strawberries is from the runners which are freely produced each summer particularly after the plants have finished fruiting. Take only one or two from each plant and any runners not required for increasing stock should be removed, otherwise they will be taking the plant's strength unnecessarily.

Use really healthy plants for propagation, and the gardener who maintains a healthy humus-rich soil that is, the compost grower, is more likely to have a healthy stock of strawberry plants than the one who relies on artificial and chemical fertilizers. There is now so much virus disease in strawberries that one cannot recommend gardeners to propagate ordinary garden stock. Unfortunately, virus diseases work from within the plants and they cannot be sprayed with any liquid which will give immunity. One difficulty is that some varieties do not show any outward sign of being virus-infected. *Royal Sovereign* is an exception however, and suspicious-looking plants can soon be destroyed. Winged strawberry aphides flying in May and June are one of the chief ways by which virus is spread.

For commercial growers and raisers the Ministry of Agriculture each year arranges for the inspection of special stock-isolated beds, grown only for runners. Certificates are issued to the runners that reach the required standards. A list of growers of certified stock is issued each autumn and it is from such sources that new stock should be obtained. The keeping down of all aphides is the first step of ensuring that plants are free from virus diseases including those known as *crinkle* and *yellow edge*. There are various insecticides for this purpose. Although poisonous, nicotine is thoroughly effective. Mix 28 g (1 oz.) in 45.5l (10 gal.) of water with a spreader and spray on thoroughly. Nicotine sprays are best applied on warm days and the liquid should reach all parts of the plants for the pests frequently hide on the undersides of the leaves. After the spray has done its work, it evaporates and does not leave any taint. This can only be used before the plants show flower buds. At other times use derris or pyrethrum. Another effective way of controlling aphides is to use a systemic spray such as Mysotox which reaches the whole plant system so that pests sucking any part of leaf or stem are destroyed.

One way of encouraging the stock plants to produce sturdy runners from late July onwards is to mulch the soil around the plants and up to 38–45 cm (15–18 in.) from them with up to 13 mm (½ in.) of compost or moist peat. Then when the runners develop they soon root and become established.

If, once the new plantlets have formed at the end, they are pegged down, the close contact with the soil or peat will encourage them to root quickly. Runners can also be rooted directly into small pots. For these use the J.I. Compost 2 or better still make up a mixture consisting of one part each sedge peat, good loamy soil and silver sand. Make sure this mixture is damp before filling the pots and sinking them up to their rims all round the healthy parent plants. As the runners develop peg one down into the centre of each pot.

Once the runners are well-rooted, and this will be obvious from their appearance, whether in pots or the open ground, sever the stolon about 13 mm (½ in.) from the pot. There will then be no check and the new plants can be moved to their fruiting positions without drawback.

Another advantage in raising pot plants is that they can be moved to bigger pots and eventually be used for forcing in the greenhouse. Whether in the open ground or in pots the young plants should be kept growing steadily and never lack moisture in summer thus avoiding any check. All runners not needed for propagation should be nipped out cleanly while small.

The remontant or perpetual-fruiting varieties can be propagated by runners, but sometimes very few, occasionally none are produced. In such cases the plants can be divided. Since the remontants are valued particularly for autumn fruiting it is advisable to pinch off the flower buds in summer in order to encourage runner production.

Strawberries in Barrels

By no means an entirely new idea, the growing of strawberries in barrels provides an interesting and often profitable means of obtaining fruit, being particularly valuable where space is restricted or where there is no garden at all. It also gives less active gardeners the pleasure of growing plants with the minimum of attention, while the control of weeds and pests is easy.

The first essential is to obtain a good barrel. Avoid those which have contained creosote or similar substances which might prove harmful to plant life. Use a barrel in which the holes, 5–6 cm (2–2½ in.) in diameter, have already been drilled, and if it is made of oak, chestnut or similar wood it will ordinarily last for years.

The barrels can be painted almost any colour and they can be used for prominent positions where they will cause interest. To render the barrels weatherproof for a long period, two under-coatings of paint are recommended before the final hard gloss colour is applied.

Stand the barrel in bricks, so that water can run away through the drainage holes in the bottom. When commencing to fill the barrel place a 15 cm (6 in.) layer of brickbats or stones at the base, to prevent the soil becoming sour through bad drainage. Then commence to fill in with a soil mixture, which for preference, should consist of three parts loam, one part good leaf mould, half part each granulated or similar peat and silver sand. To this mixture add about 680 g (1½ lb) of bone meal and if possible, 454 g (1 lb) hoof and horn manure and 454 g (1 lb) of wood ash to each barrel of compost, thoroughly mixing all in a semi-dry state. These organic fertilizers will gradually release their food value over a long period.

If desired some form of water conduit can be placed down the centre of the barrel and can easily be fixed in position by using a coil of wire netting.

If as the compost reaches each ring of holes in the barrel, some more brickbats or stones are placed in a little pile in the centre, this will provide suitable and effective drainage and also diffuse the moisture to the lower plants.

Work in the soil firmly and as each hole is reached, insert the plant roots from the outside, making sure that the growing point is left exposed and that the roots are fully spread out. Work in fine compost around them avoiding damage to the plants, when doing so. Continue to fill the barrel with soil and plants, so that each hole is occupied. On reaching the top, this too can be planted.

In regard to aftercare, nothing elaborate is needed, although it will be necessary to ensure that the central duct is kept well supplied with water and occasional applications of liquid manure will be of tremendous help to the plants being grown.

There are a number of strawberries particularly suited to this kind of culture and *Royal Sovereign* and *Cambridge Favourite* are specially good. In addition, perpetual strawberries such as *St. Fiacre* and *Baron Solemacher* are recommended. All can be planted from August until November and should yield the next year. Large sized barrels will hold 28 plants and the medium size 18, allowing for some on the top of the barrel.

Yet another advantage of growing strawberries in barrels is that they can easily be covered with netting to prevent birds from spoiling the fruit.

Strawberries under Cloches

Strawberries can be grown successfully under barn cloches. Good varieties for this work include *Cambridge Favourite, Cambridge Vigour* and *Red Gauntlet,* although *Royal Sovereign* and other varieties are also satisfactory.

Provide a well-prepared site but manuring should not be excessive. Experiments have shown that there is nothing to be gained by covering the plants too early, so that although they will have been set out in the autumn as suggested, there is no need to cloche them until mid-or late February. Runners covered earlier make too much leaf, particularly Cambridge Vigour. Cambridge Favourite and Red Gauntlet should be spaced 30 cm (1 ft.) apart in the rows. The barn type give better results than the tent cloches since the plants do not touch the glass.

Whatever covering is employed weeds almost always become

troublesome and they must be removed before they attain any great size. Some growers have found it an advantage to lay down black polythene before cloching, with holes made in it for the plants to come through.

The roots must never lack moisture, although watering must be done with great care. This applies particularly from the time the young fruits start to swell. Ventilation is also important particularly at the time the petals begin to fall. Cloches which remain closed tightly produce high temperatures and the humidity inside the cloches encourages the rapid spread of botrytis spores. These quickly settle on various parts of the plant and gain an easy hold when the decaying petals fall and remain on the foliage. It is quite a good plan to take off some of the glass during the daytime to give plenty of ventilation although steps must be taken to prevent birds from getting under the cloches.

Should botrytis appear to be gaining a hold it must be checked. A light spraying or dusting with Captan is normally sufficient to do this so long as it is used just as the blossoms begin to open. Ground beetles sometimes attack the fruit making it useless for table or market. These pests feed by night, while during the day they hide in the soil. They are most active between April and June just when the fruit is coming into its best. Draza dust placed inside the cloches but not on the plants or fruit, is usually effective.

Aphides may settle on the plants and these too must be prevented from gaining a hold. A spraying of one of the systemic insecticides usually clears these pests. As an alternative, Malathion or Metasystox can be used although it is better and safer to rely on a derris- or pyrethrum-based insecticide.

Varieties

The following are among the older varieties which are rarely grown at the present time.

Black Prince was introduced in 1837. Fairly small, it is early, a free bearer and useful for forcing as well as outdoor culture. When ripe the fruit is rich burgundy colour and of delicious flavour.

British Queen was for long among the best of all but is rarely to be had to-day. The bright scarlet fruit is of irregular shape, juicy and rich in flavour.

Dr. Hogg is of exceptional flavour. Hardier than British Queen it is not such a reliable grower.

Elton was once much used for jam-making. A hardy, vigorous-growing late sort it is hardly every heard of to-day.

Hautbois is an unusually coloured strawberry being a dark mulberry shade.

James Veitch carries enormous fruit of good flavour.

Louis Gauthier is a very pale pink, of good size but rather watery, this however, is off-set by its strong pine flavour which also belongs to the old *White Pine* sort. Both of these varieties make excellent jam, although this is of rather a tawny colour instead of the typical rich red shade we associate with strawberry jam.

President which is still sometimes obtainable produces large handsome highly-flavoured berries whether grown outdoors or under glass.

Sir Joseph Paxton was for long most widely grown. The large bright crimson fruit with solid flesh is richly flavoured. When ripe, the whole berry is of even shape. It was once much used for market, since it frequently coloured before it was ripe and therefore travelled well, while it was also valuable for forcing.

Viscomtesse de Thury is another highly-flavoured sort, being a free bearer, a compact grower and specially useful for jam.

Other varieties little grown to-day include; *Oberschlesion* a strong growing mid-season, *St. Fiacre* a hardy, good flavoured sort, and *Perle de Prague* which has never really been popular, although it is a good growing early sort, since the fruit is soft and small.

Madame Kooi is a late variety which crops heavily, the berries are often very large but it is of poor quality and flavour. *Tardive de Leopold* is a late heavy-cropping sort, with large berries and a good all-round variety. *Waterloo,* another late, produces in abundance deep red berries of fine flavour. *Madame Lefevre* is one of the best of the very early sorts doing well in the open or under cloches and dutch lights. It is a strong grower and a good cropper.

Varieties which are now widely cultivated include the following;

Royal Sovereign is undoubtedly the best known strawberry in cultivation today and is sometimes referred to as the Queen of Strawberries, holding the foremost place as a dessert variety. In addition, it is suitable for jam-making and canning being of firm texture and unique flavour. Unfortunately in recent years it has suffered enormously through virus diseases so that it is essential to obtain stocks from virus tested plants to prevent disappointment and loss later.

Alpine Strawberries

Although alpine strawberries are much smaller than the standard varieties they are well worth cultivating. They will grow in partially shaded situations particularly if the soil contains plenty of compost, peat or other humus-forming matter. They are splendid for edgings and should be spaced 30 cm (12 in.) apart with 45 cm (18 in.) between the rows. The fruit is borne on erect stems clear of the ground and is not attacked by birds.

If the first flush of flowers is picked off, the plants will crop heavily from August to October a time when the larger strawberries have finished. Propagation is from seed sown in trays of J.I. Seed Compost, or a similar mixture, in spring, or the plants can be divided after flowering making sure that each split portion is healthy with one or two strong buds.

Baron Solemacher is the best known variety. It crops heavily over a long period, the smallish dark red fruits having a buttery texture. There is also a white form.

Red Alpine Improved is also excellent and said by some gardeners to be better than Solemacher.

Alexandria has larger fruit and does well in pots. None of these produce runners.

Remontant or 'perpetual' varieties which bear large fruits from September onwards include: *Hampshire Maid,* excellent for dessert and jam; *Red Rich,* strong-growing with dark red berries; *Sans Rivale,* vigorous, heavy cropping often going on until late November; *St. Claude*, sweet, juicy and disease resistant and *St. Fiacre*, one of the earliest fruiting remontants.

Climbing Strawberries

At one time quite a lot was heard of the so-called climbing strawberries. This is really a misnomer since there are no actual climbing

[84]

varieties for none have tendrils. One or two of the remontant sorts produce long stolons on which develop a number of little plants. If these stolons are trained in an upright fashion they can be used to cover low walls, fences, lattice-work or similar supports. The top growth will die down in late autumn.

Summer-fruiting strawberries

Cambridge Favourite One of the most widely grown mid-season varieties. A heavy cropper, resistant to disease. Moderate flavour, some large fruits, mostly medium. Very suitable for preserving and freezing.

Cambridge Premier Very early, large fruits. Particularly suitable for early forcing under cloches.

Cambridge Prizewinner A first early variety for outdoor cultivation. A moderate cropper.

Cambridge Vigour A second early, bearing bright, shiny, medium-sized fruits in its first year, thereafter tending to be rather small. Good flavour. Early-autumn-planted maidens produce several trusses of fruit in the following season.

Domanil A very promising new late mid-season variety from Belgium. Heavy cropping, with an exceptionally high proportion of large, firm berries. Excellent flavour. Highly recommended.

Elista Mid-late, medium fruits, good for fresh eating or jam. A compact growing plant useful where space is limited, as plants may be set 23 cm (9 in.) apart without overcrowding.

Gigana Second early. Good cropper for its season. Berries rather hidden, large size, flavour quite good. Not suitable for bottling or freezing.

Gorella Second early. Good cropper for its season, large size, moderate flavour.

Grandee An outstanding and popular early-summer fruiting variety, producing giant-sized, well-flavoured berries up to 8 cm (3 in.) in diameter and 3 oz. in weight. It crops heavily, especially in its second year. A certain winner at the fruit shows.

Litessa A most promising new variety from West Germany. Mid-late season, heavy cropper, medium to large, very good flavour.

Merton Dawn Late mid-season. Heavy cropper, berries well displayed, moderate flavour. In appearance almost identical to Cambridge Favourite, but in official trials the yield has been greater.

Montrose Late mid-season, heavy cropper, berries medium to large, flavour quite good. Does well under cloches.

Red Gauntlet Heavy cropper. Berries well displayed, large size, fair flavour. Usually produces an autumn crop especially where it has been forwarded in spring by cloches. Some resistance to disease.

Talisman Late mid-season. Heavy cropper in its first year, berries medium to large, excellent flavour. Berries mostly medium to small in the second year. Sometimes gives an autumn crop in a favourable season.

Tamella Maiden year, season early. After the first year of fruiting it reverts to mid-season/late, cropping over a very long period. Tamella gives a useful crop in its maiden year with late autumn planting and succeeding crops in following years are extremely heavy. The attractive looking berries maintain their yield and size even during the third year of fruiting and Tamella will out yield any known variety. Flavour very good. An all-purpose strawberry which can be used for dessert, freezing, bottling and jam.

'Perpetual-Fruiting' Strawberries

Baron Solemacher Non-running *fraise du bois* – close cousin to the Alpine strawberry. Masses of thimble-sized fruits commencing June and continuing throughout the summer until first frosts. A splendid border plant but grows best in a shady position.

Gento A superb 'perpetual-fruiting' variety with very large berries of excellent flavour. Heavy cropper on runners as well as parent plant, with its heaviest and continuous fruiting period from August until October, or even later in warm situations, if cloched. May be planted in spring or autumn, and will grow well even on lime soils which do not suit summer fruiting types. Whereas most 'perpetuals' should be cropped for one year only Gento has yielded good results in the second year also. Given adequate moisture, fruit size is maintained throughout its picking period. Even when planted in the early spring, a full crop can be expected in the same year.

Ostara A recent introduction from the Netherlands. Produces a good crop overall. Berries well displayed, small to medium size, good flavour.

Rabunda A new introduction from Holland producing a heavy crop of ample-sized bright red berries of good flavour. Probably out-yields Gento in terms of actual ripe fruit picked during August and September. A wonderful variety for the shows on account of its bright attractive appearance and regular-shaped fruits.

Trellisa A very special 'perpetual' variety that both flowers and fruits freely on its runners, which may be trained against a trellis fence (hence its name). The berries are medium to large and are produced in abundance during the late summer and early autumn.

The Verti-strawb system of culture

As a result of detailed experiments the Verti-strawb system has been evolved.

The need to obtain the maximum crop from the limitation of space in a greenhouse is well recognized. With a crop such as strawberries, especially at a time when they are most expensive to buy, any and every effort to achieve such results is commendable.

Although the name of the variety used for the first experiments has never been divulged, there seems to be no reason why *Royal Sovereign, Cambridge Favourite* and similar varieties should not be used. Originally strong medium-sized runners, probably from cold storage were used. In the early part of July, 10 cm (4 in.) diameter polythene tubing in lengths up to 7 m (21 ft.) are filled with suitable compost. These are placed or fixed on raised horizontal supports up to 3.5 m (10½ ft.) high.

Holes are punched in the tubes with a soldering iron, 15 cm (6 in.) apart. Into these holes the runners are planted. Feeding and watering by trickle drip harness are carried out for up to eight weeks, when the picking of the autumn crop begins.

After a resting period, the plants are started into growth again in early January. Warmth, water and feeding will lead to the production of flower trusses before the end of February. Fruit will be ready for picking in April, the crop continuing for months so that with the July and January plantings, fruit should be available over a very long period. Some of the earliest fruits may not be of perfect shape but the quality and flavour should not be affected. This is a novel if rather expensive way of producing strawberries but well worth pursuing by those who have or can make the right conditions.

It has been claimed that instead of the usual crop of about 340 g (¾ lb) of fruit from each plant, on the Verti-strawb system, up to 1.36 kg (3 lb) per plant can be obtained – and in a limited space. The fruit will be clean, free from weather, bird and slug damage. The sun-lounge or sheltered patio can also be use for the Verti-strawb system.

Verti-strawb kits will be coming on to the market and undoubtedly many gardeners will want to use them.

STRAWBERRY TREE *(Arbutus unedo)*

In spite of its common name this subject is in no way related to the well-known strawberry. It is actually an ornamental tree which has the unusual habit of bearing both flowers and strawberry-like fruits during late autumn and early winter when few other plants are decorative. The flowers which appear one year produce the ripe fruit of the following year.

A hardy subject it will grow in all types of well-drained soil and does not object to lime. It is suitable for both small or large gardens since it will stand quite hard pruning and can be kept to a height of 3–4 m (9–12 ft.)

The rather rough bark of the trunk and stems is a pleasing reddish-brown shade, deepening to an attractive cinnamon colour when wet. Against the evergreen foliage, both the clusters of creamy-white flowers and the fruits which change from lemon-yellow to orange-scarlet, are always a source of admiration. The fruit is edible and is used in Portugal and elsewhere for making 'brandy'.

Good deep soil, firm planting and watering as necessary, will help in getting the strawberry tree established. In windy positions, a strong support should be provided although it is really best to plant where the tree will not be exposed to winds or to severe frosts.

Propagation is by seed sown in spring or grafting on to seedling stock.

TOMATO *(Lycopersicon esculentum)*

Natives of South America, these plants came to Britain in the seventeenth century when they were cultivated as ornamental subjects

[88]

under the name of 'Love Apples'. For a time they were regarded with suspicion, since some people believed them to be poisonous. Since they are semi-tropical plants they naturally like warm conditions.

The fruit contains vitamin C, although the juice of the fruit is less valuable than that of black currants, strawberries or oranges. Vitamin B1 is also present, but it is their vitamin A content that makes tomatoes so valuable.

Whether they are to be grown outdoors or under glass, the plants are raised in a similar way. Commercial growers sow from December onwards where fruit is required from the end of May. The majority of gardeners sow from early February to the end of March and fruit from these plants matures from the middle of April onwards. These sowings are for plants for fruiting in the heated greenhouse. For fruiting outdoors, seed should be sown the first week in April in the south, the third week in April in the north. Seedlings are usually ready for pricking-out fourteen days from date of sowing. The plants are gradually hardened-off for putting outdoors at the end of May or early June. Never buy plants from an unknown source.

The seeds are large and can be handled individually. They should be spaced 12 mm (½ in.) apart in boxes or pans of the John Innes or a similar seed compost. Cover the seeds well, then place glass and paper over the boxes to exclude light.

For quickest results keep the receptacles in a temperature of 18°-20°C. (65°-70°F.) After a few days, growth will be seen and the covering can be removed. Once the seed leaves open, each seedling can be transferred separately into small pots or soil blocks.

When they have settled in the pots, the temperature can be reduced by several degrees with free ventilation. Only first class seedlings should be potted up. Plants with fern-like leaves are known as rogues or jacks and should be discarded.

A good way of producing really strong plants is to maintain a fairly even temperature. When the heat varies, irregular growth is produced. Sturdy, short-jointed plants of a deep green colour are likely to be the most fruitful. Avoid long-jointed, hard, wiry-stemmed plants.

Tomatoes grow well in the warm greenhouse where there is good ventilation, a minimum night temperature of around 12°C. (55°F.), and an absence of draughts. For preference, use a greenhouse glazed to ground-level if the plants are to be grown in the 'floor' or border. Otherwise the beds will have to be raised or made up on the staging. Alternatively, grow the plants in large pots or deep boxes.

All tomato plants like fairly rich root conditions. Strawy horse manure is ideal. Where this is difficult to obtain, good substitutes used by growers are wheat straw, well-dusted with hoof and horn manure, ripe compost, well-decayed seaweed or spent hops. Peat or leaf mould help to increase the humus content and provide bulk which encourages plenty of good roots to develop. Add lime as necessary.

At planting time make sure the sub-soil is moist. Beds on the staging can be made up with the same soil mixture. First place asbestos or similar covering over the slats, followed by a layer of drainage material. Boards 23–25 cm (9–10 in.) wide should be fixed to the front of the staging to get the proper root depth when the compost is added. This need only be 13 cm (5 in.) deep at first. More compost is added as growth proceeds, so that the soil level comes to within 25 mm (1 in.) of the top of the board.

Liquid manure should be given at ten-day intervals once the first trusses of fruit have set. For plants in pots or boxes, a simple soil mixture on the basis of the John Innes potting compost No. 2 can be used. keep side-shoots removed. The number of trusses allowed will depend on the strength of the plants and how strongly they continue to grow and set fruit.

Tomatoes can be grown successfully in frames of various kinds, while barn cloches are also suitable. Place these structures in a fairly open yet sheltered position, preferably running north and south. This will encourage good growth.

In unheated greenhouses and frames, planting is usually done during mid-April, ripe fruit then being available from July onwards. A bed of fairly rich soil should be made up, well-moistened peat being useful for encouraging a good root system. Supports will be needed. Short sticks can be used but later, bigger stakes will be necessary. Keep the frame covered until June giving plenty of ventilation in both frame and greenhouse whenever the weather is favourable. Plants under tall frames can be supported by wire or string and canes.

Tomatoes do well under cloches in a sunny site and where there is shelter from winds. Excepting in light soil, take out a trench 18 cm (6–7 in.) deep and 30 cm (12 in.) wide at the top tapering at the bottom. Prepare early, applying good organic fertilizer and plenty of peat at the base to provide proper growing conditions.

Diseases

Grown under good, clean, healthy conditions the tomato is not particularly subject to diseases and disorders but it is just as liable to be affected as other plants if such maladies gain a hold on other plants growing nearby.

Among the troubles, especially under glasshouse culture, none are less understood and perhaps of more trouble in reducing yields than those of virus origin. This is partly because in spite of prolonged trials and investigations, their origin and development are complicated and difficult to recognize and control.

There are a number of distinct viruses liable to affect tomatoes and some of the more common have been given easily remembered names such as *mosaic, aucuba mosaic, fern leaf* and *streak.* It is not easy to identify these different forms and they are generally grouped together and referred to loosely as 'viruses'.

Various ornamental plants as well as weeds, may act as carriers since they are subject to the same strains of the disease. Clean seed is obviously necessary to start with.

Some authorities believe that contact between the roots of young plants, slightly damaged when planting, and the remains of a previous mosaic-affected crop are responsible for a new outbreak, for the virus is persistent in remaining on old roots a long time. It is also resistant to heat and is able to withstand a temperature of 76°C. (169°F.) for some minutes, which means that soil-steaming must be thoroughly done if the disease is to be eliminated. The same applies if formaldehyde is being used.

There is reason to believe that virus-infected seed is a source of disease, especially as tomato mosaic has appeared where circumstances preclude the possibility of soil infection. A much more widely recognized source of the disease in young plants is from tobacco transmitted by the fingers, knives and other implements, gloves and clothes used by workers handling the plants. Almost all smoking tobacco contains viruses and tests have shown that there is a definite connection between smokers and virus infected plants.

Tomato mosaic is a highly infectious and readily carried in tiny quantities of sap from diseased plants.

Cucumber mosaic is rather more virulent. The leaves show a light mottling similar to that of the tomato mosaic, but they soon develop a fern-like appearance. Growth becomes hard and thin, the fruit rarely sets properly and any which does, fails to swell. Although one may rogue-out obviously affected specimens, the disease is likely to spread, in which case plants should be destroyed.

Another virus disease is known as *streak*. This is seen first as tiny yellow mottlings on the leaves. These spread to the stems and brown markings develop, often spreading to the fruit which becomes pitted.

Spotted wilt is another form of virus disease. It is seen in the younger leaves, by their very dark colour. They begin to curl and there is little growth. Affected plants should be burned and the greenhouse fumigated with nicotine shreds or a B.H.C. Smoke Bomb. If not checked, spotted wilt can easily spread to decorative greenhouse plants.

Inter-veinal chlorosis is caused by the inability of the roots to obtain all the nutrients they need for balanced growth. Plants need nitrogen, phosphates and potash, plus calcium and other trace elements, including magnesium. All are usually present in good soil. If the roots are sluggish the leaves become discoloured between the veins and often appear patchy and pitted too. A pinch of magnesium sulphate applied to each plant and watered in well should ensure that the new leaves are healthy.

Leaf mould (Cladosporium fluvum) This is probably the most common of all tomato diseases. The air-borne spores can be very destructive once they attack a plant and often destroy the whole leaf system if left unchecked.

This disease first appears as pale grey spots and markings on the undersides of the foliage. Affected areas are soon changed to a purplish shade and then to brown, the upper surface of the leaves also shows deep discolouration which spreads.

Infection often takes place when the plants are smaller, the disease being favoured by stagnant, poorly-ventilated conditions and spreading most rapidly on cold house plants and where heat has been discontinued during summer months. To stop the trouble, improve ventilation and spray the plants with a good fungicide such as benomyl.

It is necessary to keep the air moderately dry and in the bigger greenhouse, the opening of both side and roof ventilators will keep the air moving in all parts of the greenhouse. Avoid watering in late afternoon and even in summer, if just a little heat is maintained it prevents stagnant atmospheric moisture which is liable to encourage the disorder.

Where the disease is troublesome year after year, it is advisable to grow mould resistant varieties of which there are now a number. Some are more resistant than others and it seems possible that there are several forms of leaf mould, since some varieties are more susceptible than others.

Blight (Alternaria solani) This is similar to potato blight and probably comes from the same or a similar fungus. It does not appear in all seasons and seems almost entirely confined to outdoor plants. It rarely appears before mid-July and is seen by the greyish-brown or blackish markings on leaves, stems and sometimes fruits. It is most likely to occur during damp close weather and can usually be checked by spraying with Bordeaux Mixture or a similar fungicide at ten- to fourteen-day intervals.

Didymella lycopersici This is a disease which attacks the stems at soil level and subsequently spreads higher up the stem. Although it is similar to botrytis there are no grey mould growths. A soil-borne disease, it will if unchecked soon spread through a batch of plants. Infected specimens should be burned and the soil sterilized before any other crop is planted. Ster-izal watered into the ground will usually check the infection if used when only one or two plants in a batch are affected.

Sclerotinia rot This shows itself by the mass of fluffy white, soft outgrowths on the stem at soil level. This subsequently dries and becomes hard and black. Remove and burn plants immediately the disease is seen. If left, the spores re-enter the soil to continue their destructive work. Soil sterilization is the only means of controlling this disease apart from moving the soil and replacing it with fresh material.

Bacterial canker Although not common this needs to be dealt with, without delay. It is seen as dark brown or black streaks on the stems which as the disease progresses become channelled causing the collapse of the plant. Soft growth induced by the use of quick-acting fertilizers or fresh manure renders plants more prone to attacks. Burn affected plants and sterilize the soil before replanting.

Foot rot (Phythium) This disease or group of diseases may attack plants in the seedling stage. Often known as 'damping off' and collar rot, it affects seedlings and sometimes older plants at or just above soil level. As a result, the stem shrivels and the plant wilts and topples over. Sometimes a whole batch of plants will become affected and the seedlings collapse in a few hours. Damping off thrives under damp, stuffy conditions and is most liable to attack seedlings sown too thickly or which have become drawn through lack of light or when the soil is packed down and not aerated.

Where the trouble has been prevalent in the past, the use of steam-sterilized soil reduces the possibility of its recurrence. Affected plants cannot be cured and should be burned with a little of the surrounding soil. Then apply a solution of Cheshunt Compound which will stop the spread of the disease. If this solution is used to 'water' the boxes or pots at the time of sowing it acts as a protection to the seedlings.

Verticillium wilt This is another soil-borne disease the spores of which enter the roots and prevent the plants from receiving moisture and food supplies. The stem becomes hard and discoloured while the lower leaves in particular appear to droop and bunch with quite severe wilting in warm weather.

The leaves recover their normal appearance once there is reduced transpiration at nightfall. Yellowish patches may form on the leaves which take on a greyish appearance and growth is retarded. If only one or two plants become infected, it is best to burn them, but where a whole batch is attacked a deeper secondary root system should be encouraged to develop by mulching the plants with a good layer of moist peat.

Once the secondary roots are penetrating the soil well the plants can be fed and watered normally. A very weak solution of Ster-izal fluid applied at seven- or eight-day intervals until the secondary root system is working well will check the activities and spread of verticillium wilt.

Burn all plant remains when the plants have finished cropping. It is to overcome verticillium disease that grafted plants are sometimes grown.

Canker (Botrytis cinerea) This is one of the most common diseases affecting tomatoes being most likely to occur in cool or low temperatures where the air is stagnant and moisture-laden. Although it can attack leaves and fruit it is best known as a stem disease. It is when side-shoots and leaf stalks are not cleanly removed that the fungus spores are liable to grow in the wounds, as they will if the stem is bruised or cut.

Leaves may rot and the air-borne spores sometimes settle on the fruit causing pale green, slightly raised circular workings usually referred to as botrytis spots, which look as if they are water-soaked. Often these spots are contained in themselves and do not spread. At other times they cause the rotting of the whole fruit. Sometimes the spores fall on the calyx and the fruit falls just as it has set.

Since botrytis can be so destructive, every effort should be made to provide free air circulation which means regular attention to ventilation which will prevent excessive humidity. Dusting plants with Folosan is effective if used at the first sight of botrytis or better still, if used as a routine method from late June onwards.

Greenback is a physiological disorder in which the area around the stalk of the plant remains green or pale yellow and refuses to ripen. Lack of potash is a frequent cause, while erratic watering and long exposure to direct sunshine encourages the trouble. There are now a number of non-greenback hybrid varieties available.

Blossom drop is sometimes a nuisance. The flower stalks turn yellow at the knuckle and the flowers fall. It is often due to a dry atmosphere or the inability of the roots to take up moisture.

Blossom-end rot can also spoil a crop. It is chiefly due to unbalanced growth and shortage of water at a vital time in the development of the fruit. The damage is seen at the base or flower end of the fruit. This at first appears to be bruised, but then becomes black and leathery. Correct watering and an adequate potash supply minimize the possibility of blossom-end rot.

Buck eye rot This disorder of the fruit is due to careless watering leading to disease spores from the soil being splashed on the lower fruit. These organisms are held in a film of water. They germinate and cause greyish-brown lesions with dark brown concentric rings developing into the shape of an animal's eye. Affected fruit should be collected and burned and care taken to prevent water splashing on to the fruit.

Fruit cracking is caused by irregular water supplies. The fruit skin hardens when moisture is short. When water is available later, the sudden swelling of the fruit breaks the skin. The remedy is obvious. Heavy feeding with nitrogenous fertilizers is also a cause of fruit cracking.

Grafting Tomato Plants

The practice of grafting tomatoes has now become firmly established and is proving to be highly successful in combating common root diseases such as corky root or root rot, nematodes (root knot eelworm), verticillium and fusarium. There are three strains of rootstock seed known as follows: Root Stock 'KN' resistant to corky root or root rot and nematodes; Root Stock 'KVF', resistant to corky root, fusarium and verticillium; Root Stock 'KNVF', resistant to corky root, verticillium, fusarium and nematodes.

How to Graft

Two lots of plants have to be grown, the root stock and the fruiting variety (all the standard and well-known varieties will graft). Seed of the root stock is somewhat slower to germinate and should be sown a few days earlier than the fruiting variety. The germinating temperature should be 18°–20°C. (65°–70°F.). When seedlings have reached the well-expanded leaf stage, they are ready for pricking out into seed trays. From this stage they must be grown with enough room to allow for the development of a good sturdy plant so that twenty-four plants to a standard size seed tray is ample. When seedlings are established after pricking out, they should be grown on in a lower temperature of 13°–15°C. (56°–60°F.)

Plants are ready for grafting when 10 cm (4 in.) tall and have a good stem thickness. Lift the plants from the trays for the grafting operation, cut off the top of the root stock plant at a point to leave one or two leaves, next make a downward cut half an inch long and not quite half-way through the stem. A razor blade is the best tool for a clean non-bruising cut. The same length upward cut is now made in the plant of the fruiting variety, in this case the top of the plant must not be cut off.

Next fix the cut lips neatly into each other holding them firmly to allow an assistant to make one simple wrap at the union with three-quarter inch wide transparent adhesive tape.

The pair of plants now joined by the graft are potted as one plant with both root systems intact and grown on in the normal way until large enough for planting out. Plant out as for ordinary grown plants and with both root systems intact. (Except in case of 'KVF' — for these it is necessary when the graft has taken, to cut away the root of the fruiting variety at a point just below the graft, so that the roots cannot transmit sap poisoned by verticillium and fusarium to pass up the stem.)

Pests

Although pests can become troublesome both in the greenhouse and outdoors, if tomato plants are grown under hygienic conditions and the plants are examined frequently there is no need to be unduly concerned.

Well-grown healthy plants are less likely to fall prey to pest attacks than those which have not had care, or where the soil lacks humus or has been continually dosed with artificial fertilizers.

Whitefly This is a tiny moth-like pest which settles on many greenhouse plants as well as on outdoor crops particularly in mild weather. They suck sap from the leaves in the same way as greenfly. They exude honey-dew on which moulds develop making leaves and stems sticky and unsightly. The way to keep the pest in check is to spray with a B.H.C. or parathion wash or to use a modern smoke bomb insecticide. Various pesticides including malothion, parathion and resmethrin are often used. Fairly recently biological pest control has been relied on by commercial and private growers. A parasite, *Eucaisia formosa* is usually supplied as black parasitized scales on 'cards' or tobacco leaves. Use them as soon as whitefly are seen. Directions are supplied with the parasites which should not be used where infestations are already established.

Red Spider This tiny reddish-brown pest attaches itself to the undersides of the leaves producing whitish specklings on the upper sides. Left unchecked the pests settle on the growing points and may make a fine web-like growth over them.

Although Volck is first class for use as a spray, killing both the insects and their eggs, the liquid works by contact. This is why some growers of greenhouse plants prefer to use an aerosol or smoke bomb which reaches all parts of the plants as well as the crevices of the greenhouse.

Leaf Hoppers Although these attack a wide range of plants they are not serious pests for the tomato. Their chief danger is in eating into the cotyledon of the seedlings resulting in unbalanced growth. Nicotine or similar fungicides applied in a temperature around 18°C. (65°F.) is the main means of destroying the pests.

Thrips These are minute winged pests which sometimes attack tomatoes in the seedling stages causing discolouration or loss of leaves. This can lead to stunted growth. In serious attacks parathion smoke fumigators will eradicate the pest.

Greenfly Although these are among the worst of plant pests they are not usually serious in tomato plants. If they do become established they cause foliage distortion and if they attack the fruit while it is tiny irregular markings may develop. The most serious effect of these aphides is that they can easily become virus carriers. There are many greenfly insecticides which are most effective and can be used on tomato plants without any adverse effect.

Woodlice These are a menace only in the early seedling stages. Then they often damage the plant stems and sometimes bite right through it at soil level. Derris and Parathion will readily destroy woodlice. Make sure that hiding places are not provided for them by leaving rubbish lying about.

Leaf Miner This pest marks the foliage with the feeding punctures of the flies, and the tunnelling markings of the maggots, readily seen between the leaf tissues. This means that ordinary insecticides will not reach the maggots and although it is often possible to destroy these in the leaf with finger and thumb if they persist nicotine wash or fumigation becomes necessary.

Cutworms It is rarely that these pests are troublesome and then only on outdoor crops. When they attack they bite the stem at soil level causing the plant to collapse.

Leather jackets These too, cannot be regarded as a serious tomato pest and the damage they do is similar to that done by cutworms.

[98]

Wireworm dust or B.H.C. dust will usually destroy both.

Wireworms These pests will often burrow into the stem at soil level completely stopping the growth of plants. They are more likely to be present outdoors on land recently turned over from grass. Wireworm dust or naphthalene dust should be worked into the soil before putting in the plants.

Symphalids are small white pests which attack the roots. Soil sterilization has little effect. Plants should be drenched with parathion or Gamma B.H.C. two or three days after planting out.

Planting outdoors

Considering their origin, tomatoes are most accommodating plants but when they are grown outdoors, a really good start under the right conditions is essential to secure complete success.

Since they are frost-tender, weather conditions and the state of the soil must be such that growth continues unchecked once the plants have been placed in the open ground. It is not wise to do this until quite the end of May. In northern districts or exposed places, early June is soon enough.

One very cold night with cutting winds can soon spoil a batch of well-grown plants. Wherever possible, advantage should be taken of the shelter of a wall or fence. A tall growing crop such as runner beans also gives protection. Such shelters not only stop the checking effect of winds but they reflect additional heat and assist fruit ripening.

The preparation of the site needs to be done well in advance of planting. Deep digging and the working in of decayed manure and garden compost are invaluable. Bone meal is a great help in providing feeding material so long as it is applied at least three months before planting outdoors. Do not use fresh manure since this encourages soft, lush growth.

Just before planting some growers work into the top soil moistened peat and an organic fertilizer such as Maxicrop or fish manure. The extra humus matter encourages a stronger and larger fibrous root system which is so essential for the production of a good crop. The site should be well drained, which greatly lessens the possibility of root disorders.

Plants must be thoroughly hardened off before being planted out. Make sure they are well watered some time before they are knocked out of their pots. Set them 45 cm (18 in.) apart allowing 60 cm (2 ft.) between rows. With large plantings leave an alleyway of 90 cm–1.2 m (3–4 ft.) after every four rows. This makes it easier for cleaning the soil, side-shooting and fruit gathering.

Plant with a trowel and press the soil firmly around the roots so that they are in close contact with the soil. Do not water the plants unless the surrounding soil is on the dry side. If the weather turns cold as soon as the tomatoes have been put out place cloches, large pots or newspapers over them at night but remove them in the morning.

Plants selected for growing on should be short-jointed, stocky, of good colour and about 20–23 cm (8–9 in.) high. Leggy specimens will never make good plants. It is best to place supports in position before planting. This ensures the roots are not damaged and the plants will be kept upright. If they fall about, the stems may become 'kinked'. As the plants grow keep them tied to the supports with soft string or wide raffia. Leave room in the tie for the stems to expand. Where really large, heavy trusses of fruit develop, these too should be looped to the main stem to prevent breakage of the truss stem. Remove all side-shoots while they are small.

Hot days followed by warm, humid nights are the ideal requirements for the full natural setting of the fruit. In hot, dry weather light overhead sprayings of water can be given in the evening, but do this with care to avoid the crippling blight disease.

Some gardeners now use hormone setting sprays when atmospheric conditions are unsuitable for natural fertilization or where growth is rank and the flowers fail to set fruit. With good culture these helps should not be necessary, but it is important to get the bottom truss of fruit to set for this encourages even, healthy growth and improves both the quality and setting tendency of later trusses.

Avoid letting the soil dry out and then flooding with water. Such a happening leads to irregular growth as well as cracked fruit. A surface mulching of peat, leaf mould, or similar material will help to maintain a cool root run liked by the plants, as well as preventing the surface soil from drying out.

On deep, well-prepared land, artificial watering will seldom be needed. If it can be avoided so much the better, for continued watering brings the roots near the surface, where they suffer from dryness much more than when they are deep in the soil. In addition, watering produces a high humidity which from early July onwards, predisposes the plants to attacks by blight.

If the soil has been well prepared and enriched, it should be unnecessary to give extra feeding, but should growth become extra luxuriant and rank, a dressing of seaweed manure scattered round the plants and watered in, will help to steady growth.

Outdoors it should be easily possible to bring three trusses of fruit to maturity. If the position is warm and sheltered and the weather good, a fourth truss can sometimes be allowed. There is no point in allowing plants to waste their strength on growth and flowers from which it is impossible to secure fruit. When the chosen number of trusses has been selected, the plants should be stopped at one leaf beyond the top truss and from that time, one or two side-shoots can be allowed to develop. This will keep the sap flowing and discourage fruit-splitting which sometimes occurs once the plants have been stopped. The excess of sap then goes into the fruit, which cannot expand fast enough, causing the skin to crack, particularly if heavy rains follow a period of dry weather. At this time too, any lower discoloured leaves can be removed, as can odd leaves, which will improve air circulation as well as helping to lessen the possibility or spread of blight.

Gather the fruit as soon as it is well-coloured, in some districts birds will peck the fruit once it is tinted. Often they are only seeking moisture, so that it is helpful to place saucers or similar containers of water near the plants. I have found this to work among other crops, both vegetables and flowers which birds sometimes attack, particularly during spells of hot, dry weather.

If at the end of September some of the fruit is still unripe, the complete trusses should be cut off and hung up in the warm greenhouse or living-room. Alternatively, the fruits can be gathered individually and wrapped in paper and placed in a drawer or box where the warmth and darkness will bring out the colour. Kept in this way, ripening fruit can be had over a period of several weeks.

Ring Culture

The ring culture of tomatoes is now widely practised. It is a method which provides controlled conditions of nourishment and water supply. It was first seriously practised at the Tilgate Horticultural Research Station in Sussex.

Because of indifferent crops then being produced, it was decided to grow greenhouse tomatoes in some large bottomless earthenware rings or containers. These rings were filled with compost and planted in the usual way. By chance some of the rings had been placed on a tile floor such as found in old conservatories and growing rooms, and some or part of the floor had been covered with ashes from a coal-fired boiler.

It was found that the plants standing over the ash grew much more freely and cropped much more heavily. Since all plants were grown in the same compost and had the same attention no answer could be at first found for their greatly differing results.

It was not until the rings were moved that it was discovered it was the plants that had grown over the ash base that had fruited so heavily. They had made a strong secondary root system in the ash layer which had remained damp allowing the roots to spread out widely. The plants standing over the tiles had their roots restricted to the rings.

Since that discovery fresh advances have been made in ring culture. Rings of greatly different materials have been used and apart from weathered ashes many other materials have been employed on which to stand the rings. These layers have become known as aggregates, and among the other aggregates now used are small grade clinkers, sand, crushed ballast, and peat. Gravel can be used but is not so moisture-retentive as the other materials. The same applies to stone chippings and very coarse clinkers. The depth of the aggregate is not important except that it should not be less than 10 cm (4 in.) although there does not seem any advantage in going beyond 15 cm (6 in.)

It is not essential to put down polythene or anything else before putting down the aggregate, but where in the past there has been trouble from disease or eelworm, an effective way of isolating the aggregate layer from the greenhouse soil is to first provide a layer of polythene, or concrete may be laid down for a permanent separation. In this case some provision must be made for the escape of surplus water, although the aggregate must be kept constantly moist so that the secondary zone of roots never dries out. Any possibility of waterlogging resulting in unhealthy root action must be avoided.

Where there is sufficient height tomatoes can be grown in rings on greenhouse benches although provided shade is given the plants can be trained to the roof. There is no problem in growing tomatoes in rings in the open ground, although it is best to select a south-facing site. If the aggregate layer is raised a little above the surrounding soil it prevents compost being washed into or rain beaten over the aggregate. Alternatively boards can be placed round the aggregate to keep it intact.

The John Innes Compost No. 3 has been found very suitable for ring culture. It was in fact used in the initial trials and properly made it is not so liable to dry out as 'ordinary' composts which are often too light depending on the type of loam used. This perhaps is not so important once the secondary roots in the aggregate are working well, if they are not and the feeding roots in the rings dry out the foliage may wilt and some of the flowers may fall before they set fruit. It is unwise after having carefully prepared the aggregate site and used the right material, to use 'any old soil'. To do so would be to ask for trouble and an indifferent crop.

With regard to the size of the rings. It is now possible to buy a number of types of bitumized cardboard and similar material. A good size is 20 cm (8 in.) deep with a top diameter of 23 cm (9 in.). Having made a 5–8 cm (2–3 in.) layer of compost firm on the bottom of the ring (placed on the aggregate) the tomato plant should be taken from its pot and placed firmly in the ring pressing the soil closely around the ball of roots without damaging them. Bring the soil to within 38 mm (1½ in.) of the top of the ring, this space being left for initial waterings and feeding.

Then give a good watering so the roots settle in their new compost. After about ten days, water should be applied close to the plant stem, (this is ball watering) and the aggregate should be made wet and kept so. After a month or so, the roots will be penetrating the aggregate and ball watering should cease. All moisture then being drawn through the secondary root system. By this time the nutrients in the rings will be almost exhausted and feeding into the rings at seven-day intervals should be commenced.

Do not water into the rings after feeding until it is evident the compost is becoming dry. The lack of free moisture in the container causes the foliage to droop a little and lose its fresh lively colour.

It is always best to feed in solution, since with the comparatively little actual watering of the rings, there is less opportunity for the solid feed to be carried to the fibrous roots.

The fertilizer first used on tomatoes grown in rings was known as 667 from the analysis of 6% each of nitrogen and phosphoric acid and 7% potash which provides the necessary magnesium for good colour. Once the first truss has set the liquid fertilizer should be given at seven-day intervals. It is now possible to obtain a number of really good non-forcing fertilizers with a similar analysis. One must bear in mind that plants in rings do require more feeding than those in the border. Otherwise they become half-starved, growth is indifferent, and the quality and quantity of the fruit poor.

The removal of side-shoots and general attention needed by tomatoes in rings is the same as required by plants grown under the usual method.

Outdoor ring culture is carried out in the same way as with the greenhouse plants, although it is helpful if the sides of the aggregate layer in the bushes prepared for the plants is protected by boards or bricks to keep it in position. The aggregate is made up in the manner indicated earlier, and the rings filled with the appropriate compost placed 38–45 cm (15–18 in.) apart. It is unwise to plant until well into May the exact time depending on weather conditions. Some growers avoid wind or late frost damage by erecting hessian around the rows or cloches, or other glass structures can be placed over individual plants. In this way an early crop can be produced.

Supports should be given as soon as plants go into the rings and nothing is better than strong bamboo canes and green fillis, although the square rose supports are quite satisfactory.

By whatever methods tomatoes are grown regular side-shooting is necessary and a watch kept for aphides and other pests. It is essential to encourage the first truss to set otherwise the plants grow leggy. Apart from the necessity of a moist atmosphere if the plants or their supports are given a sharp tap it does help to distribute the pollen leading to fertilization.

Straw Bale Culture

The technique of growing tomatoes on straw bales has grown out of work done some years ago at the Lee Valley Horticultural Experimental Station in Hertfordshire. It is a process which can be carried out by the amateur gardener without difficulties.

Among basic advantages of straw-bale cultivation is the isolation from soil-borne troubles of which tomato mosaic virus may be among the most important. Root debris from a previous crop is also known as a source of disease infection not always entirely eliminated by the general methods of soil sterilization.

Start with a bale of clean straw. Place this broadside downwards in the soil border of the greenhouse, or to provide extra headroom for plants in a low house, the bale can be sunk by removing up to 60 cm (2 ft.) of soil. If the bales are laid flat on sheets of thin gauge polythene extending 15 cm (6 in.) beyond the sides of the bales it helps to prevent infection of the straw from the soil. Soak the bale with frequent drenchings of water over a period of two or three days. Pierce the straw with a sharp rod of some kind to aid water penetration. If hot water can be applied, this softens the straw more quickly.

Fertilizer must then be applied evenly. For each hundredweight of straw, you need 2 lb nitro-chalk, 1¼ lb triple superphosphate, 2¼ lb potassium nitrate and ¼ lb magnesium sulphate. Mix all these together, spread evenly on the top of the bale and water-in gradually. Alternatively, some growers use 2 lb nitro-chalk and 3½ lb well-balanced fertilizer to each bale.

A greenhouse temperature of around 10°C. (50°F.) is needed to induce fermentation. After a couple of days the straw will begin to heat, rising to 38°–49°C. (100°–120°F.) Ammonia fumes will be given off and plants must not be brought into the greenhouse too soon or they will become scorched.

The next step is to make a 'trough' 15 cm (6 in.) deep, 30 cm (12 in.) wide, down the centre of the bales, or separate stations 15 cm (6 in.) deep and 30–38 cm (12–15 in.) apart each way are suitable. Fill these with good compost such as J.I.2 and allow this to warm through for a couple of days before setting out the plants. The heat produced in the bales tends to dry out the straw and compost quickly. Daily watering of the straw and rooting soil is needed. Roots develop very quickly and so long as they never lack moisture, the plants make vigorous growth. The usual method of supporting the plants is needed with individual canes or by string fixed to the rafters and round the plant stems. Since the bale sinks as it decomposes, do not tie the plants too tightly. Ventilation is also important.

Once the first truss of fruits can be seen, the plants should be given liquid feeds every fourteen days. Choose a feed fairly high in potash since the decomposing straw will provide all the nitrogen needed. Another advantage from the decomposing straw is that there is an escape of carbon dioxide which aids the production of heavier crops.

Bale-grown plants are subject to pest attacks as well as air-borne fungus spores, which means that they must be looked over frequently so that any disorders of pests can be dealt with before they gain a hold. No trouble should occur from root rot, verticillium or soil nematodes, which is one of the main reasons for growing tomatoes on bales. Comparison tests have shown that bale culture properly carried out does produce a heavier crop from healthier plants although extra lime has to be given to the regular watering and feeding processes.

Once cropping has finished, the decomposed straw becomes an excellent source of humus-forming organic compost. This can be well forked into the garden beds and borders and around fruit trees and bushes.

Apart from the use of straw bales, experiments have been made in the growing of tomato plants on shallower beds of straw, made of wads about 20 cm (8 in.) in depth. These trials have shown that it is possible to obtain greater yields of early fruit through higher plant population in the greenhouse.

Among successful experiments made is the planting of four rows of plants on straw wad beds of 20 cm (8 in.) deep and 1.35 m (4½ ft.) wide. This works out at 35 cm (14 in.) apart in and between the rows. This closeness of plants could mean overcrowding. To avoid this, plants in the two outer rows in each bed are stopped and side-shoots kept removed, when the third truss of fruit has set. The two inner rows can be allowed to produce up to seven or eight trusses.

Adventurous growers might even try growing a second crop in the same season on the old straw beds. The plants can go in as soon as the earlier plants have finished cropping, which from an early sowing should be by the middle of July, growing the plants in the same way in respect of planting and stopping.

Not all growers will want to experiment in this intensive method but there is no reason why ten or more plants should not be grown on individual straw wads. A generous feeding programme will have to be followed, using non-forcing fertilizer, so that growth is steady and the fruit colours well.

The Tom-Bag

One of the latest successful methods of growing tomatoes is by the Gro-Bag or Tom-Bag system. The bags used contain tomato compost which is specially formulated to produce the right type of good, firm, close-jointed growth, with broad dark green leaves and well-developed flower trusses. This tomato compost contains all the necessary major, minor and trace elements, both in available and slow release forms, and in the correct balance with the emphasis on potash, to give the tomato plants a good start and encourage the development of high quality sound, firm fruit.

It is normal to grow four plants in each standard bag of which the size is 1.1 m long, 38 cm wide and 15 cm deep, for a long-term heated crop, and five plants for short-term or cold house growing with five or six trusses.

Raise the tomatoes in the usual way and before planting 38 cm apart, shake the compost evenly along the bag which should be placed level and square up the sides. To form a single row, lay the bags end to end. Cut out the panels along the dotted lines to form a mini-trough, leaving the cross-bands to support the sides.

Place the young plants with the minimum of firming. Water thoroughly to moisten *all* the compost in the bag. String the plants (with a non-slip loop, tied around the stem below the first leaf) to the overhead wire, and twist plants round the string in a clockwise direction. Canes should *not* be driven through the bags. Horizontal wires at 30 cm intervals in length are ideal. Well-fed plants carry heavy crops and must be properly supported.

Varieties

Extensive comparative trials are conducted by horticultural firms and private individuals annually. New varieties are regularly introduced but some of the older sorts are still dependable. The following are all first class.

Ailsa Craig Heavy cropper of remarkable flavour.
Alicante One of the best for under glass and outdoors.
Big Boy Produces enormous fruits weighing up to 680 g (1½ lb).
Carter's Fruit Peels like a peach. For indoors or outdoors.
Craigella Very early, heavy cropping, small fruit.
Eurocross (F.1. hybrid). Early maturing indoor variety.
Gardener's Delight A small fruiting outdoor variety of sweet flavour.
Golden Queen Yellow fruiting, for both indoors and outdoors.
Harbinger An old variety for under glass and outdoors.
Kirdford Cross (F.1. hybrid). Compact very disease resistant.
Outdoor Girl A very early outdoor variety.
Ronaclave (F.1. hybrid). An early outdoor, heavy cropping, variety.
Sonato (F.1. hybrid). A disease resistant non-greenback F.1. hybrid
Tangella Fruits of intense tangerine colour.
Tigerella A novelty variety with red and golden stripes for under glass or outdoors.

Dwarf varieties include; *The Amateur, French Cross* (F.1. hybrid), *Sigmabush, Sleaford Abundance* and *Tiny Tim,* the latter growing only 30–38 cm (12–15 in.) high, being very suitable for window-boxes or pots.

Pixie is a new variety which can be sown in succession indoors over a very long period growing well on window sills and in tubs or boxes.

VEITCHBERRY

This hybrid is the result of a cross between Raspberry November Abundance and a wild blackberry. The large, early-ripening fruit has a sweet and really delicious taste. In addition the reddish-purple canes are quite ornamental in winter when often there is little other colour in the fruit garden.

[108]

WHORTLEBERRY *(Vaccinium myrtillus)*
This genus includes both deciduous and evergreen shrubby plants useful for their fruits and tinted autumn foliage. They bear racemes of little bell-shaped flowers in early summer. Of the deciduous species, *Vaccinium myrtillus* is good. Growing about 45 cm (18 in.) high, it is a heath-like shrub with small ovate foliage and sprays of pendant pink flowers which are followed by showy bluish-black, round, edible fruit which is valued for whortleberry pie, and when topped with cream, cannot be resisted. This subject is also known variously as bilberry, blaeberry and blueberry although the true blueberry is *Vaccinium corymbosum*.

All vacciniums thrive in moist peaty, but lime-free soil and are best transplanted in March or April. Old, badly-placed stems should be cut out in late winter or early spring.

Propagation is from half-ripened cuttings 8–10 cm (3–4 in.) long-inserted under glass where there is bottom heat, in late July or August. Other means of increasing stock are by off-sets, divisions, layering in autumn or by seed sown as soon as ripe in early autumn. *Vaccinium vitis-idaea* is the cowberry often seen growing wild. This is a low-growing evergreen of spreading habit, the red fruits being edible.

WORCESTERBERRY *(Ribes divaricatum)*
For long this subject has been regarded as a hybrid between a gooseberry and a black currant but this is not so. Certainly the fruit resembles both these subjects, being smaller than a gooseberry and usually bigger than a black currant, the flavour being similar to both. The berries are borne in clusters the colour being deep reddish-purple often becoming almost black. They are useful for jams and jellies.

A native of North America, it has been known in cultivation since 1826 and in an old book on 'trees and shrubs', it is described as being common on the banks of streams near many Indian villages.

The name 'worcesterberry' was given to the plant by a Mr Parsons who had once been employed by Messrs. Rowe, Nurserymen of Worcester and who subsequently traded on his own account.

The strong-growing stems are quite closely furnished with thorns which undoubtedly is one reason why the worcesterberry has never become very popular. The general treatment regarding culture and pruning is the same as recommended for gooseberries. Soil in good condition, well drained but moisture-retentive and containing plenty of humus matter is ideal. Propagation is by cuttings in autumn or early spring.

YOUNGBERRY

This is a good hybrid raised by a Mr Young of California by crossing a dewberry with a phenomenal berry. The large fruit is of splendid flavour containing few seeds and small core. As the berries ripen they change from deep red to black, giving a pleasing appearance. The fruit is produced on little stems away from the canes making it easy to gather although fortunately, the vigorous stems have few thorns. Since the plants are of a semi-trailing habit they should be planted at least 2 m (6 ft.) apart, selecting a site which does not dry out. Well drained, yet moisture-retentive soil encourages heavy cropping.

Propagation is simple by layering the tips of the long stems, which are easy to pin down into the soil. Once rooted, the tips can be severed and grown on individually.

Chapter Six: Harvesting, Storing and Freezing Fruit

Considering the care with which most gardeners grow their fruit bushes it is surprising how indifferent many of them are to the way in which they gather the crop. Careless picking not only impairs the keeping of the fruit but is likely to damage the bushes and sometimes the following season's crop too.

The colour and general appearance of the fruit is a good guide in determining when the crop is really ready for harvesting, although in gardens one need only pick the fruit as it ripens whereas on a commercial basis it is customary and labour-saving to clear the crop in one or two pickings.

Black currants are often deceptive when it comes to judging ripeness. Some berries look ripe before they are ready for gathering and it is wise to test them first.

Red and white currants should be evenly coloured before being picked and unless currants are required for immediate use they should not be gathered when wet or they will deteriorate quickly.

Gooseberries do not all ripen at the same time and so the bushes need 'going over' several times. If required for dessert the fruit should be fairly ripe, for bottling or canning it should be firm and for jam it need not be in quite such good condition.

Raspberries are fit to eat when they part easily from the core and need regular picking since birds and maggots soon find them.

Blackberries and loganberries should be gathered while firm and strawberries as soon as evenly-coloured otherwise slugs and birds will discover them.

It is only recently that the freezing of fruit has become worthwhile.

Unless you are able to grow your own soft fruit it is doubtful whether it is advisable to attempt the venture, for to be successful, the crop should really be put in the freezer within an hour or so of picking.

Gooseberries and bilberries are fairly reliable since they are firmer than most other soft fruits. Blackberries, strawberries, loganberries and raspberries all of which should have their hulls removed lose their taste and break down quickly once taken out of the freezer. These, with black, white and red currants as well as bilberries, can be packed in sugar.

Gooseberries should be topped and tailed before being put in a thin syrup.

When freezing tomatoes use firm just-ripe fruits of medium size. While they can be frozen whole or halved, so they can be used for grilling, some of the flavour is lost. It is better to make tomato *purée*. For this, peel and cut up the fruits quickly, otherwise they become a watery product. When taken out of the freezer remember to season the *purée* before serving.